MAP SYMBOLS

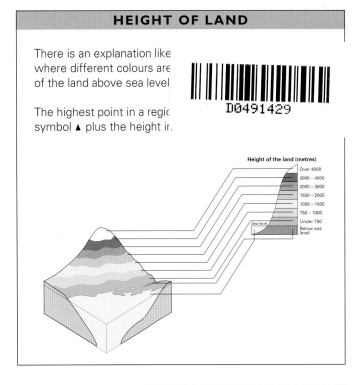

- Sea
- Coastline
- Airport
- Cape name
- Colours showing the height of the land
- Country name
- River
- National boundary (international boundaries are shown as ━━━━)
- Lake
- Line of longitude
- High point, with height in metres
- River name
- Name of mountain range
- Regional name
- Main railway
- Main road
- Sea feature name
- Line of latitude
- Symbols indicating towns: the larger the population of the town, the larger the symbol

HEIGHT OF LAND

There is an explanation like where different colours are of the land above sea level

The highest point in a region symbol ▲ plus the height in.

Height of the land (metres)

Over 4000
3000 – 4000
2000 – 3000
1500 – 2000
1000 – 1500
750 – 1000
Under 750
Below sea level

Sea level

SCALE BAR

Every map has a scale statement, scale bar and ruler accompanying it. For a full explanation of scale and how to use the scale bar, see page 2.

Scale 1:48 000 000   1 cm on the map = 480 km on the ground

0	960km	1920km	2880km

cm   cm

SCALE COMPARISON MAP

This map, or one of the U.K. and Ireland, appears on most of the maps of the continents at the same scale as the main map. They give an idea of the size of that continent.

England and Wales on same scale

LOCATOR MAP

There is a small map such as this on every map page. The bright green area shows how the main map fits into its larger region.

Philip's World Atlases are published in association with The Royal Geographical Society (with The Institute of British Geographers).

The Society was founded in 1830 and given a Royal Charter in 1859 for 'the advancement of geographical science'. Today it is a leading world centre for geographical learning – supporting education, teaching, research and expeditions, and promoting public understanding of the subject.

Further information about the Society and how to join may be found on its website at: **www.rgs.org**

PHOTOGRAPHIC ACKNOWLEDGEMENTS
Alamy /Roger Bamber p. 24 (centre), /Stocktrek Images, Inc. p. 36; **Corbis** /Tim Graham p. 24 (bottom), /Reuters p. 44, /Royalty Free p. 73; **Crown Copyright** p. 7 (map extract); **Eurostar** p. 26; **Fotolia.co.uk** p. 76; **Fugro NPA Ltd** pp. 8, 9, 10, 12, 26, 27, 37, 49, 60, 61, 74, 78, 79; **iStockphoto.com** p. 24 (top); **Patricia and Angus Macdonald** p. 7; **NASA** p. 11; **Precision Terrain Surveys Ltd** p. 6.

Ordnance Survey®   Page 6: The Edinburgh city plan is based on mapping data licensed from Ordnance Survey® with the permission of the Controller of Her Majesty's Stationery Office. © Crown copyright 2009. All rights reserved. Licence number 100011710.

COPYRIGHT PHILIP'S

TYPES OF SCALE

In this atlas the scale of the map is shown in three ways:

WRITTEN STATEMENT

This tells you how many kilometres on the Earth are represented by one centimetre on the map.

1 cm on the map = 20 km on the ground

SCALE RATIO

This tells you that one unit on the map represents two million of the same unit on the ground.

Scale 1:2 000 000

SCALE BAR

This shows you the scale as a line or bar with a section of ruler beneath it.

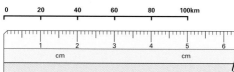

HOW TO MEASURE DISTANCE

The map on the right is a small part of the map of Southern Europe, which is on page 34 in the World section of the atlas.

The scale of the map extract is shown below:

Scale 1:10 000 000   1 cm on the map = 100 km on the ground

To measure the distance from London to Paris you can use any of the three methods described above.

For example:

USING THE WRITTEN STATEMENT

Using the scale above, you can see that 1 centimetre on the map represents 100 kilometres on the ground.

Measure the distance on the map between London and Paris. You will see that this is about 3.5 centimetres.

If 1 cm = 100 km

then 3.5 cm = 350 km (3.5 x 100)

USING THE SCALE RATIO

Using the scale above, you can see that the ratio is 1:10 000 000.

We know that the distance on the map between the cities is 3.5 cm and we know from the ratio that 1 cm on the map = 10 000 000 cm on the ground.

We multiply the map distance by the ratio.

= 3.5 x 10 000 000 cm
= 35 000 000 cm
= 350 000 m
= 350 km

USING THE SCALE BAR

We know that the distance on the map between the cities is 3.5 centimetres.

Measure 3.5 cm along the scale bar (or use the ruler as a guide) and read off the distance in kilometres.

Using these three methods, now work out the distance between London and Cardiff on the map above.

The map on the left is an extract from the map of Asia on page 39 in the World section of the atlas. Below, you can see the scale of this map. See if you can calculate the distance between Kolkata and Bangkok.

Scale 1:48 000 000   1 cm on the map = 480 km on the ground

DIFFERENT SIZES OF SCALE

The table on the right shows the distances from London to Paris and Bangkok to Kolkata on the maps on page 2. The map distances are both 3.5 centimetres, but the distances on the ground are very different. This is because the maps are at different scales.

Included on most of the continent maps, in the World section of this atlas, are **scale comparison maps**. These show you the size of the UK and Ireland, or England and Wales, drawn at the same scale as the main map on that page. This is to give you an idea of the size of that continent.

	Map Distance	Map Scale	Distance on the Ground
London – Paris	3.5 centimetres	1:10 000 000	350 kilometres
Bangkok – Kolkata	3.5 centimetres	1:48 000 000	1,680 kilometres

Below are three maps which appear in this atlas:

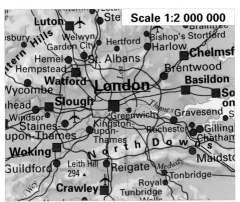

Scale 1:2 000 000

These maps all show London, but the map above shows much more detail than the maps on the right. The map above is a larger-scale map than the maps on the right.

Scale 1:7 500 000

A **large-scale** map shows more detail of a **small** area.

A **small-scale** map shows less detail of a **large** area.

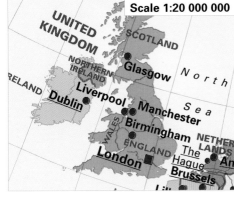

Scale 1:20 000 000

Notice how the scale ratios at the top right of each map are getting larger as the scale of the map gets smaller.

DIRECTION ON THE MAPS

On most of the atlas maps, north is at the top of the page. Lines of latitude cross the maps from east to west. Longitude lines run from south to north. These usually curve a little because the Earth is a globe and not a flat shape.

POINTS OF THE COMPASS

Below is a drawing of the points of a compass. North, east, south and west are called **cardinal points**. Direction is sometimes given in degrees. This is measured clockwise from north. To help you remember the order of the compass points, try to learn this sentence:

Naughty **E**lephants **S**quirt **W**ater

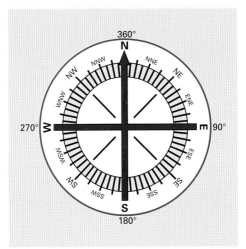

USING A COMPASS

Compasses have a needle with a magnetic tip. The tip is attracted towards the Magnetic North Pole, which is close to the Geographical North Pole. The compass tells you where north is. You can see the Magnetic North Pole on the diagram below.

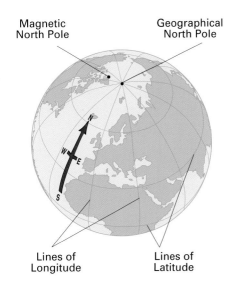

Magnetic North Pole   Geographical North Pole

Lines of Longitude   Lines of Latitude

ACTIVITIES

Look at the map below.
If Ambleside is east of Belfast then:

• Valencia is _____ of Belfast;

• Renfrew is _____ of Ambleside;

• Oxford is _____ of Plymouth;

• Belfast is _____ of Oxford;

• Plymouth is _____ of Renfrew.

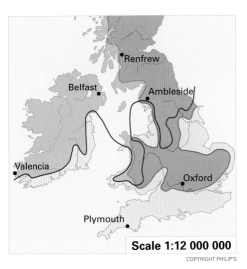

Scale 1:12 000 000

COPYRIGHT PHILIP'S

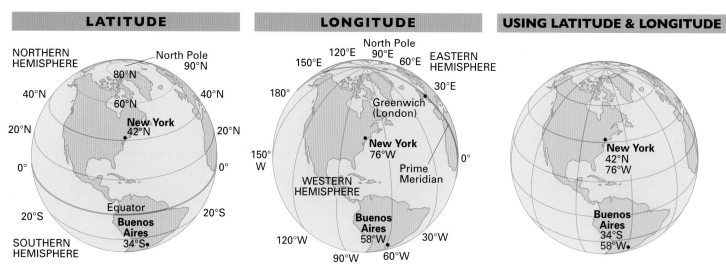

LATITUDE

NORTHERN HEMISPHERE
North Pole
90°N
80°N
40°N · 40°N
60°N
20°N · 20°N
New York
42°N
0° · 0°
Equator
20°S · 20°S
Buenos Aires
34°S·
SOUTHERN HEMISPHERE

Lines of latitude cross the atlas maps from east to west. The **Equator** is at 0°. All other lines of latitude are either north of the Equator, or south of the Equator. Line 40°N is almost halfway towards the North Pole. The North Pole is at 90°N. At the Equator, a degree of longitude measures about 110 km.

LONGITUDE

North Pole
120°E 90°E 60°E
150°E · · EASTERN HEMISPHERE
30°E
180° ·
Greenwich (London)
150° W · New York 76°W · 0°
Prime Meridian
WESTERN HEMISPHERE
Buenos Aires 58°W
120°W · · 30°W
90°W 60°W

Lines of longitude run from north to south. These lines meet at the North Pole and the South Pole. Longitude 0° passes through Greenwich. This line is also called the Prime Meridian. Lines of longitude are either east of 0° or west of 0°. There are 180 degrees of longitude both east and west of 0°.

USING LATITUDE & LONGITUDE

New York
42°N
76°W

Buenos Aires
34°S
58°W·

There are 60 minutes in a degree. Latitude and longitude lines make a grid. You can find a place if you know its latitude and longitude number. The latitude number is either north or south of the Equator. The longitude number is either east or west of the Greenwich Meridian.

SPECIAL LATITUDE LINES

The Earth's axis is tilted at an angle of approximately 23½°. In June, the northern hemisphere is tilted towards the Sun. On 21 June the Sun is directly overhead at the **Tropic of Cancer**, 23°26'N, and this is midsummer in the northern hemisphere. Midsummer in the southern hemisphere occurs on 21 December, when the Sun is overhead at the **Tropic of Capricorn**, 23°26'S. On the maps in this atlas these are shown as blue dotted lines.

In the North and South Polar regions there are places where the Sun does not rise or set above the horizon at certain times of the year. These places are also shown by a blue dotted line on the maps. The **Arctic Circle** is at 66°34'N and the **Antarctic Circle** is at 66°34'S.

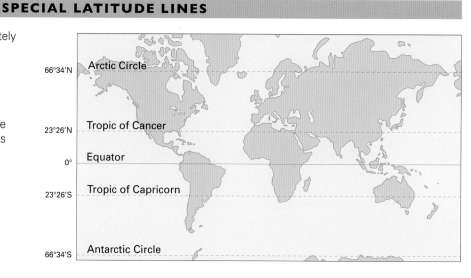

66°34'N — Arctic Circle
23°26'N — Tropic of Cancer
0° — Equator
23°26'S — Tropic of Capricorn
66°34'S — Antarctic Circle

LATITUDE AND LONGITUDE IN THIS ATLAS

In this atlas lines of latitude and longitude are coloured blue.

On large-scale maps, such as those of England and Wales on pages 16–17, there is a line for every degree. On smaller-scale maps only every other, every fifth or even tenth line is shown.

The map on the right shows the UK and Ireland. The latitude and longitude lines are numbered at the edges of the map. The bottom of the map shows whether a place is east or west of Greenwich. The side of the map tells you how far north from the Equator the line is.

Around the edges of the map are small yellow pointers with letters or figures in their boxes. Columns made by longitude lines have letters in their boxes; rows made by latitude lines have figures.

In the index at the end of the atlas, places have figure-letter references as well as latitude and longitude numbers to help you locate the place names on the maps.

On the map opposite, London is in rectangle **8M** (this is where row 8 crosses with column M). Edinburgh is in **4J** and Dublin is in **6F**.

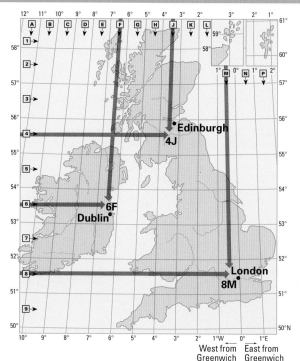

West from Greenwich   East from Greenwich

HOW TO FIND A PLACE

The map on the right is an extract from the map of Scotland on page 18. If you want to find Stornoway in the atlas, you must look in the index. Places are listed alphabetically. You will find the following entry:

The first number in **bold** type is the page number where the map appears. The figure and letter which follow the page number give the grid rectangle on the map in which the feature appears. Here we can see that Stornoway is on page 18 in the rectangle where row 1 crosses column B.

The latitude and longitude number corresponds with the numbered lines on the map. The first set of figures represent the latitude and the second set represent the longitude. The unit of measurement for latitude and longitude is the degree (°) which is divided into minutes (').

Latitude and longitude can be used to locate places more accurately on smaller-scale maps such as those in the World section. A more detailed explanation of how to estimate the minutes can be found on page 90.

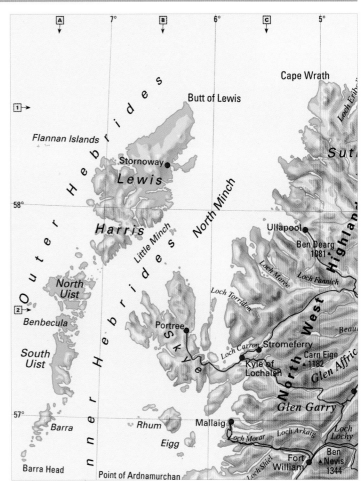

MAKING MAPS

One of the greatest problems in making maps is how to draw the curved surface of the globe on a flat piece of paper. As a globe is three dimensional, it is not possible to show its surface on a flat map without some form of distortion.

This map (right) shows one way of putting the globe on to paper, but because it splits up the land and sea it is not very useful.

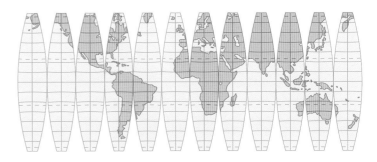

The map below is better because it shows the correct size of places. It is an **equal-area map**. For example, Australia is the correct size in relation to North America, and Europe is the correct size in relation to Africa. Comparing certain areas is a useful way to check the accuracy of maps. Comparing Greenland (2.2 million km²) with Australia (7.7 million km²) is a good 'area test'.

The map below is called **Mercator**. It has been used since the 16th century. The area scale is not equal area, but many sea and air routes are drawn on this type of map because direction is accurate. The scale of distances is difficult to put on a world map. On the Mercator map, scale is correct along the Equator but is less correct towards the Poles.

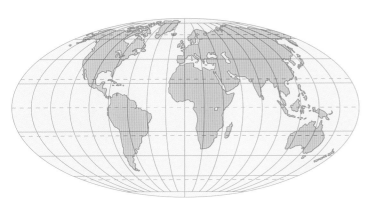

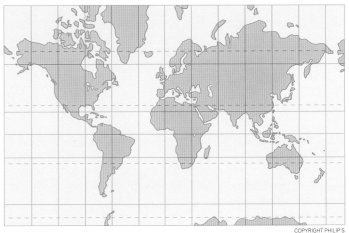

COPYRIGHT PHILIP'S

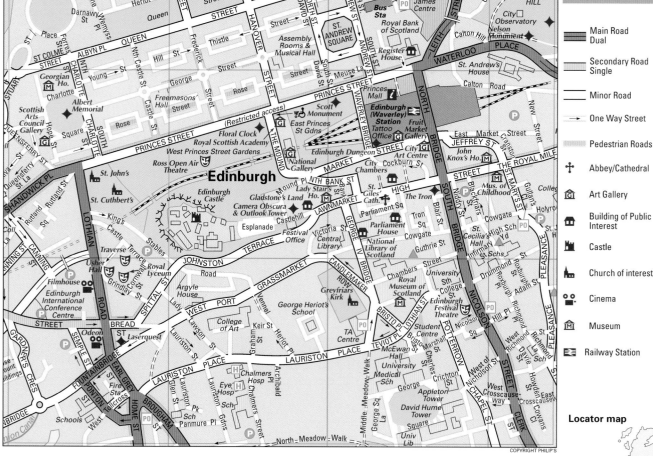

KEY TO MAP SYMBOLS

Main Road Dual	Shopping Street
Secondary Road Single	Railway
Minor Road	Railway / Bus Station
One Way Street	Shopping Precinct / Retail Park
Pedestrian Roads	Park
✝ Abbey/Cathedral	🎭 Theatre
🖼 Art Gallery	ℹ Tourist Information Centre
🏛 Building of Public Interest	✦ Other Place Interest
🏰 Castle	Ⓗ Hospital
⛪ Church of interest	Ⓟ Parking
📷 Cinema	PO Post Office
🏛 Museum	▲ Youth Hos
Railway Station	

Scale 1:10 000   1 centimetre on the map and aerial photograph = 100 metres on the ground

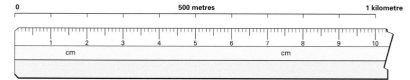

0   500 metres   1 kilometre

Locator map

Edinburgh

St Ives

KEY TO MAP SYMBOLS

A30	Main road		Other road, drive or track, fenced and unfenced
B3074	Secondary road		Path
	Road generally more than 4m wide		Footpath
	Road generally less than 4m wide		National Trail/ Long Distance Route; Recreation Route
	Single track		Cutting; tunnel; embankment
	Road over; Road under; Level crossing;		Station, open to passengers; siding
	Coniferous trees		Scrub
	non-coniferous trees		Bracken, heath or rough grassland
	Coppice		Slopes

Place of worship

Place or former place of worship	with tower	CH	Clubhouse
	with spire, minaret or dome	FB	Footbridge
	Building; important building	PO	Post office
	Lighthouse, disused lighthouse; beacon	Sch	School
	Triangulation pillar; mast	W; Spr	Well; spring

Ground survey height
Air survey height

Vertical face/cliff

Surface heights are to the nearest metre above mean sea level. Where two heights are shown, the first height is to the base of the triangulation pillar and the second (in brackets) to the highest natural point of the hill

Contours may be at 5 or 10 metres vertical interval

	Parking/Park & Ride, all year/seasonal		Camp site/caravan site
	Information centre, all year/seasonal		Recreation/leisure/ sports centre
	Museum		Golf course or links

Reproduced from the 2008 Ordnance Survey 1:25,000 Explorer Map with permission of the controller of Her Majesty's Stationery office © Crown Copyright

Scale of photograph 1:10 000

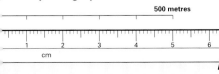

1 centimetre on the photograph = 100 metres on the ground

Scale of map 1:25 000

1 centimetre on the map = 250 metres on the ground

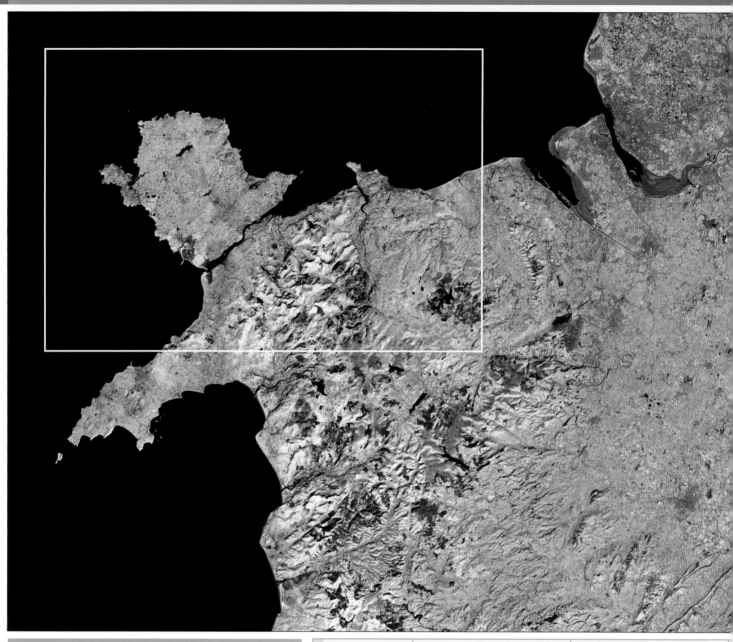

KEY TO MAP SYMBOLS

⊙ ◉ ◉ ⊙ ◎ ⊙ ○ ○   Town symbols

Built-up areas		Main passenger railways	
CONWY	Administrative area names		Other passenger railways
SNOWDONIA	National park names	⊕	Major airports
Motorways		Rivers	
Major roads		Lakes or reservoirs	
Other important roads		▲ 1085	Elevations in metres
Administrative boundaries		▪	Places of interest

Locator map

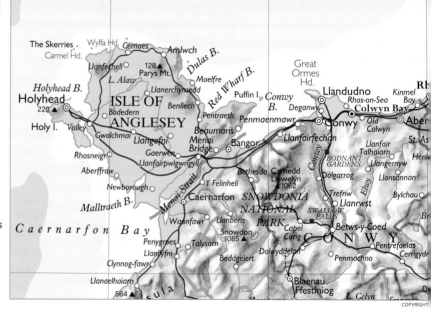

Scale 1:760 000   1 cm on the map and satellite image = 7.6 km on the ground

0	38km	76km

0 1 2 3 4 5 6 7 8 9 10
cm   cm

SATELLITE IMAGERY

images on these pages were produced by the
[Land]sat 7 satellite, launched by NASA in 1999.
[It tra]vels around the Earth at a height of over
[700] km. It is able to scan every part of the Earth's
[surfa]ce once every 16 days. The data is
[tran]smitted back to Earth where it is printed in
[false] colours to make certain features stand out.
[On] these pages grass and crops appear light
[gree]n, soils and exposed rock light grey, woodland
[dark] green, moorland brown, water black and
[built]-up areas dark grey. The image on this page
[show]s North-east England and the image on page
[8 sh]ows North Wales. Both images were
[reco]rded in late March. Comparing the maps,
[whic]h are taken from *Philip's Modern School Atlas*
[with] the images helps identify specific features on
[the i]mages.

Locator map

COPYRIGHT PHILIP'S

Scale 1:760 000   1 cm on the map and satellite image = 7.6 km on the ground

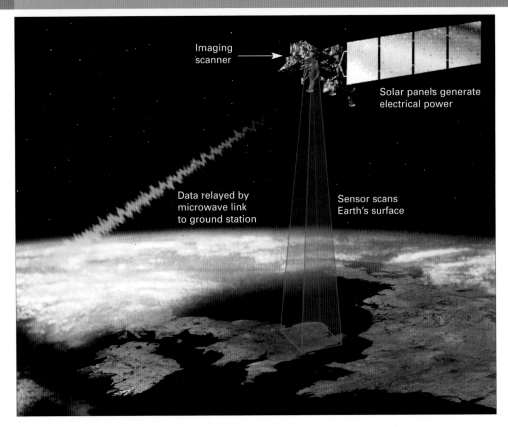

Imaging scanner

Solar panels generate electrical power

Data relayed by microwave link to ground station

Sensor scans Earth's surface

◄ **Earth Observation Satellites**

Powered by outstretched solar panels, Earth Observation Satellites, such as the one shown here, can collect and relay back to Earth huge volumes of geographical data which is then processed and stored on computers.

Depending on the sensors fitted, the choice of orbit and altitude, these satellites can provide detailed imagery of the Earth's surface at close range or monitor environmental issues covering the entire world. Objects as small as 1 metre across can now be seen from space as well as the entire surface of our planet, allowing us to monitor issues such as the atmosphere, land and sea temperature, vegetation, rainfall and ice cover.

The importance of recording this information over time is that it enables us to see long-term changes and increases our understanding of the processes involved. Some satellites have been collecting data for over 25 years. A few of their uses are shown on this page and the page opposite.

▲ **The River Thames, London**

This image shows central London from St Paul's Cathedral, in the upper left-hand corner, across to the Tower of London and Tower Bridge on the right-hand side. The image was captured from a satellite 680 km above the Earth and travelling at 6 km per second. It was captured at about midday in late October, the low sun showing clearly the shadows of the Shard and the chimney of Tate Modern. *(Image © EUSI, Inc. All Rights Reserved/Fugro NPA)*

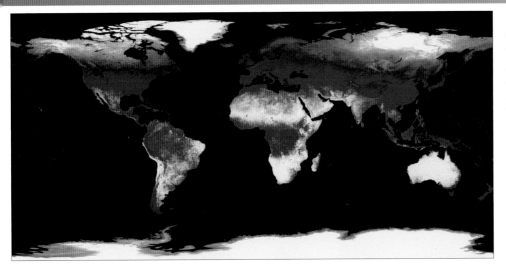

◀ **World Land Surface Temperature, November 2012**
The satellite which captured this data uses another set of sensors that enable it to capture different data and over a much wider area. The colours range from light blue, indicating −25°C, through reds and oranges up to yellow, indicating +45°C. The land surface temperature thus shows the beginning of winter north of the Equator and summer south of the Equator.

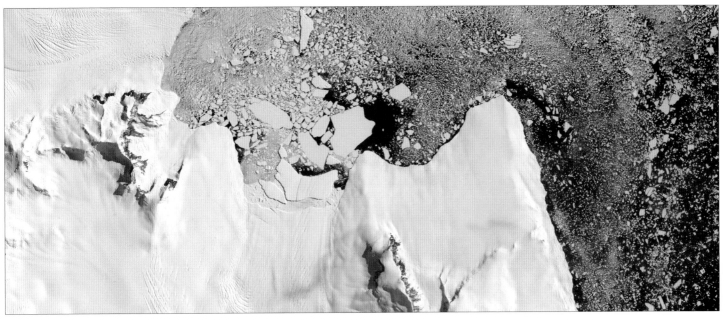

▲ **Ice Cover, Alexander Island, Antarctica**
An important use for satellites is to monitor inaccessible areas of the world that are environmentally sensitive, such as the ice caps surrounding the North and South Poles. This image shows the Hampton Glacier, which is at the foot of the image, flowing towards the sea. The ice then breaks off into a series of icebergs, which can be seen at the top. Because satellites revisit these areas regularly, changes to the extent of the ice can be monitored.

▲ **Weather**
Weather satellites travel at the same speed as the Earth's rotation and stay in daylight to allow them to monitor the same area for major storms and other events. In order to capture as much of the Earth's surface as possible, they orbit farther out in space, about 35,000 km above the Earth's surface. This image clearly shows a hurricane approaching the coast of central America and the Gulf of Mexico.

United Kingdom and Ireland from Space

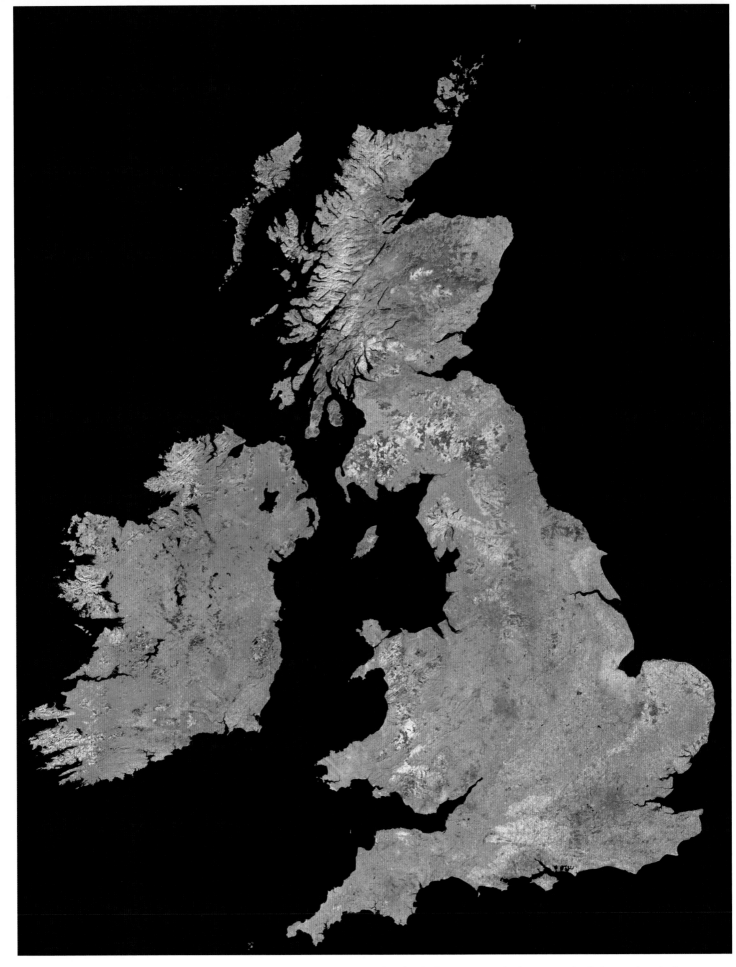

▲ The United Kingdom and Ireland, seen from Space

The colours on this image have been processed to match the natural tone of the landscape. The large amount of agricultural land in the UK is reflected by the extensive green on the image. In Scotland, the snow-covered Cairngorm Mountains can be seen, with brownish-green coniferous forests below the snow line. Most of Ireland has a mid-green colour, which indicates the presence of rich pasture.

In the west, the lighter colour indicates moorland or bare rock and is also visible in the Cambrian Mountains in Wales, the Pennines and the Lake District in England, and the Scottish Highlands. Urban areas are shown as dark grey in colour.

COPYRIGHT PHILIP'S

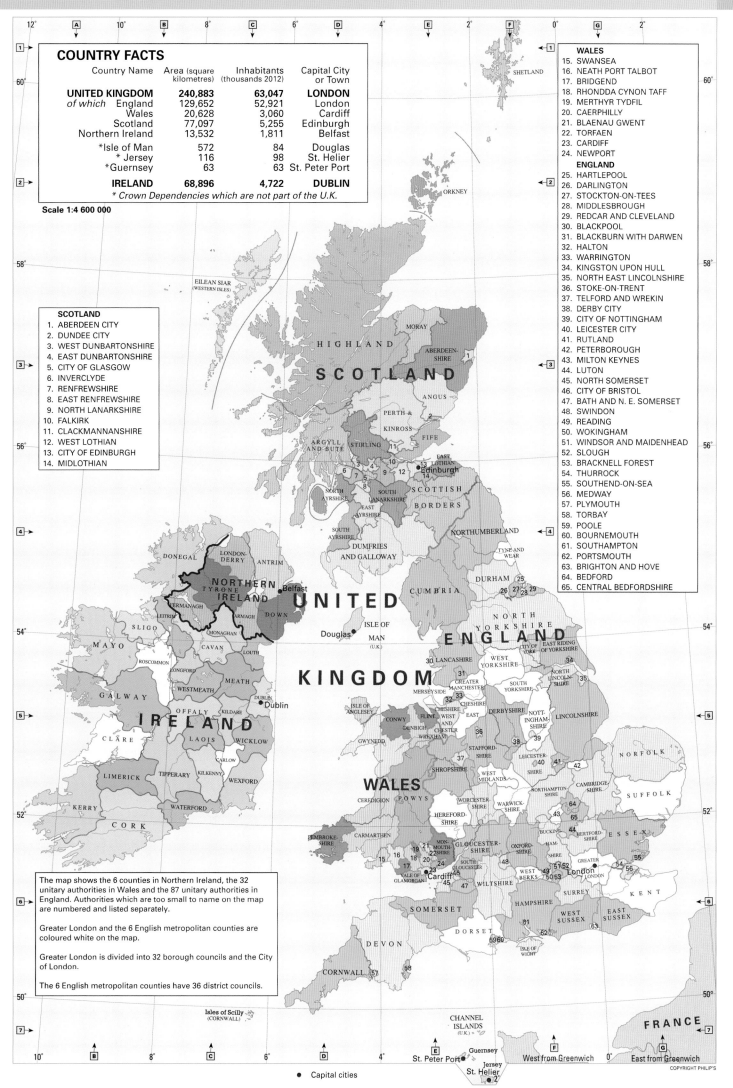

COUNTRY FACTS

Country Name	Area (square kilometres)	Inhabitants (thousands 2012)	Capital City or Town
UNITED KINGDOM	**240,883**	**63,047**	**LONDON**
of which England	129,652	52,921	London
Wales	20,628	3,060	Cardiff
Scotland	77,097	5,255	Edinburgh
Northern Ireland	13,532	1,811	Belfast
*Isle of Man	572	84	Douglas
* Jersey	116	98	St. Helier
*Guernsey	63	63	St. Peter Port
IRELAND	**68,896**	**4,722**	**DUBLIN**

* Crown Dependencies which are not part of the U.K.

Scale 1:4 600 000

SCOTLAND
1. ABERDEEN CITY
2. DUNDEE CITY
3. WEST DUNBARTONSHIRE
4. EAST DUNBARTONSHIRE
5. CITY OF GLASGOW
6. INVERCLYDE
7. RENFREWSHIRE
8. EAST RENFREWSHIRE
9. NORTH LANARKSHIRE
10. FALKIRK
11. CLACKMANNANSHIRE
12. WEST LOTHIAN
13. CITY OF EDINBURGH
14. MIDLOTHIAN

WALES
15. SWANSEA
16. NEATH PORT TALBOT
17. BRIDGEND
18. RHONDDA CYNON TAFF
19. MERTHYR TYDFIL
20. CAERPHILLY
21. BLAENAU GWENT
22. TORFAEN
23. CARDIFF
24. NEWPORT

ENGLAND
25. HARTLEPOOL
26. DARLINGTON
27. STOCKTON-ON-TEES
28. MIDDLESBROUGH
29. REDCAR AND CLEVELAND
30. BLACKPOOL
31. BLACKBURN WITH DARWEN
32. HALTON
33. WARRINGTON
34. KINGSTON UPON HULL
35. NORTH EAST LINCOLNSHIRE
36. STOKE-ON-TRENT
37. TELFORD AND WREKIN
38. DERBY CITY
39. CITY OF NOTTINGHAM
40. LEICESTER CITY
41. RUTLAND
42. PETERBOROUGH
43. MILTON KEYNES
44. LUTON
45. NORTH SOMERSET
46. CITY OF BRISTOL
47. BATH AND N. E. SOMERSET
48. SWINDON
49. READING
50. WOKINGHAM
51. WINDSOR AND MAIDENHEAD
52. SLOUGH
53. BRACKNELL FOREST
54. THURROCK
55. SOUTHEND-ON-SEA
56. MEDWAY
57. PLYMOUTH
58. TORBAY
59. POOLE
60. BOURNEMOUTH
61. SOUTHAMPTON
62. PORTSMOUTH
63. BRIGHTON AND HOVE
64. BEDFORD
65. CENTRAL BEDFORDSHIRE

The map shows the 6 counties in Northern Ireland, the 32 unitary authorities in Wales and the 87 unitary authorities in England. Authorities which are too small to name on the map are numbered and listed separately.

Greater London and the 6 English metropolitan counties are coloured white on the map.

Greater London is divided into 32 borough councils and the City of London.

The 6 English metropolitan counties have 36 district councils.

● Capital cities

COPYRIGHT PHILIP'S

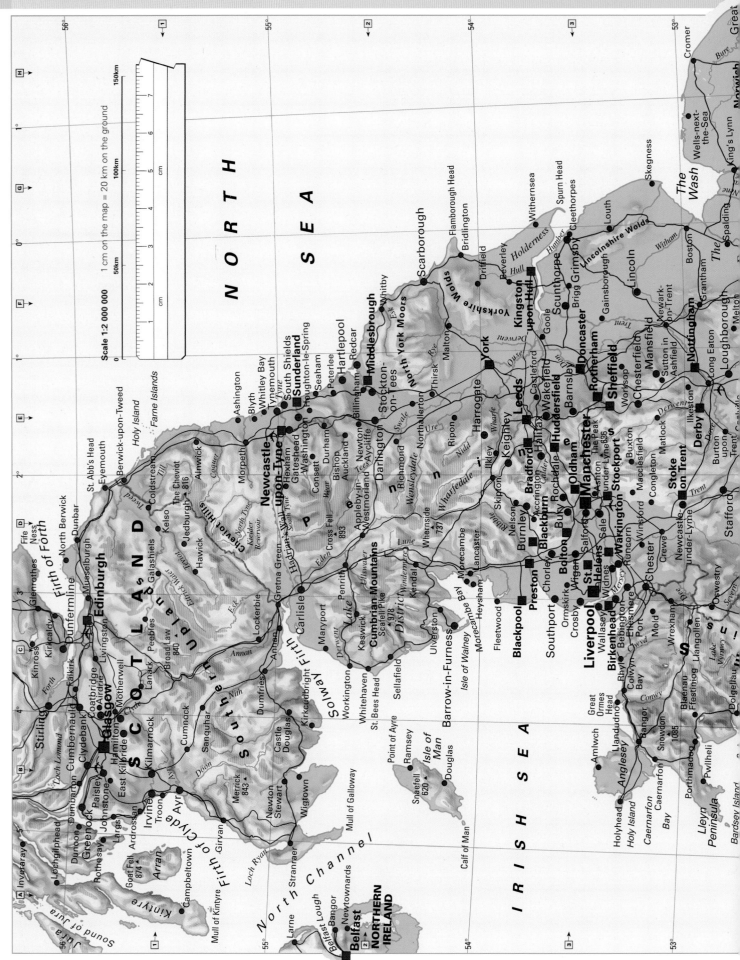

Scale 1:2 000 000   1 cm on the map = 20 km on the ground

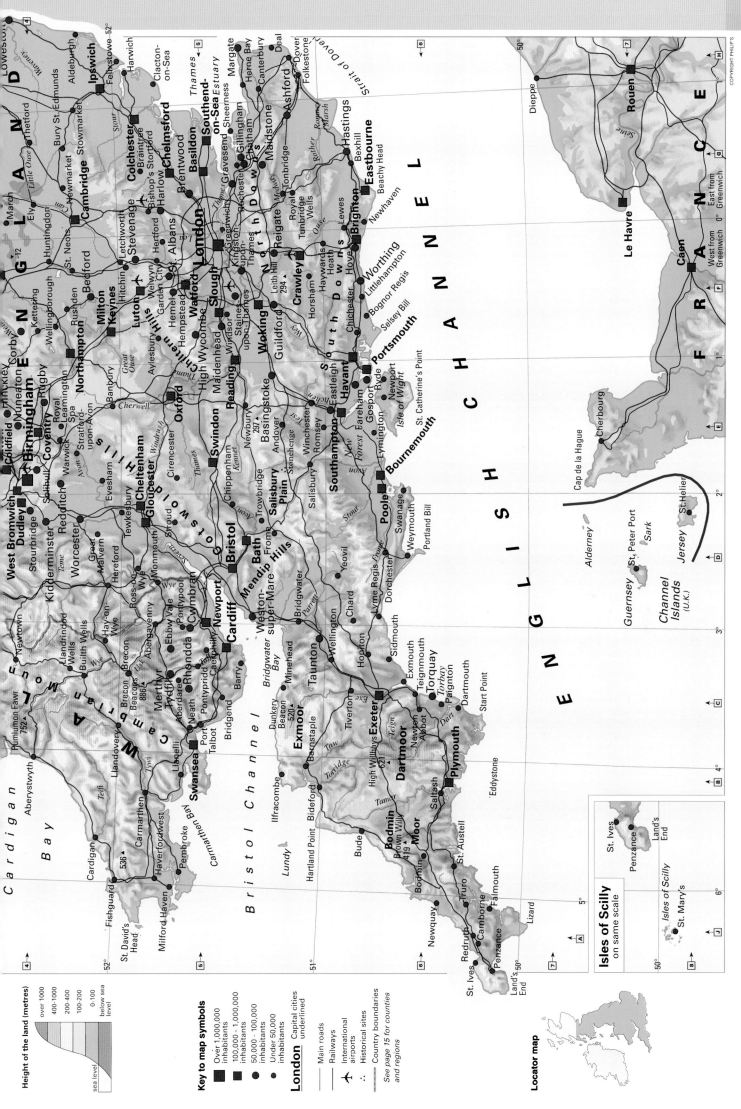

Height of the land (metres)

over 1000
400–1000
200–400
100–200
0–100
below sea level

sea level

Key to map symbols

● Over 1,000,000 inhabitants
● 100,000 – 1,000,000 inhabitants
● 50,000 – 100,000 inhabitants
● Under 50,000 inhabitants

London Capital cities underlined

— Main roads
— Railways
✈ International airports
∴ Historical sites

— — Country boundaries

See page 15 for counties and regions

Isles of Scilly
on the same scale

St. Ives
Penzance
Land's End

Isles of Scilly
● St. Mary's

Locator map

COPYRIGHT PHILIP'S

F R A N C E

Rouen
Dieppe
Le Havre
Seine
Caen
Cherbourg
Cap de la Hague

Channel Islands (U.K.)
Alderney
Guernsey · St. Peter Port
Sark
Jersey · St. Helier

E N G L I S H   C H A N N E L

E N G L A N D

Lowestoft
Wroxham
Aldeburgh
Harwich
Ipswich
Felixstowe
Thetford
Bury St. Edmunds
Stowmarket
Newmarket
Clacton-on-Sea
Thames
Margate
Herne Bay
Canterbury
Deal
Dover
Folkestone
Strait of Dover
Ely
Cambridge
Huntingdon
St. Neots
Bedford
Letchworth
Stevenage
Hitchin
Welwyn Garden City
Hertford
St. Albans
Colchester
Braintree
Bishop's Stortford
Harlow
Brentwood
Chelmsford
Basildon
Southend-on-Sea
Sheerness
Gillingham
Gravesend
Chatham
Rochester
Maidstone
Royal Tunbridge Wells
Tonbridge
Ashford
Rother
Royal Marsh
Hastings
Bexhill
Beachy Head
Eastbourne
Newhaven
Lewes
Brighton
Hove
North Downs
London
Greenwich
Kingston-upon-Thames
Slough
Watford
Hemel Hempstead
Luton
Aylesbury
High Wycombe
Maidenhead
Windsor
Staines-upon-Thames
Reading
Woking
Guildford
Reigate
Leith Hill 294
Crawley
Horsham
Haywards Heath
South Downs
Chichester
Worthing
Littlehampton
Bognor Regis
Selsey Bill
Portsmouth
Havant
Gosport
Fareham
Ryde
Newport
Isle of Wight
St. Catherine's Point
Eastleigh
Southampton
Winchester
Basingstoke
Andover
Newbury 297
Stonehenge
Salisbury
Romsey
Lymington
New Forest
Bournemouth
Poole
Swanage
Weymouth
Portland Bill
Dorchester
Lyme Regis
Yeovil
Chard
Bridport
Sidmouth
Exmouth
Teignmouth
Torquay
Torbay
Paignton
Dartmouth
Start Point
Exeter
Exmoor
Barnstaple
Bideford
Taunton
Wellington
Hopton
Tiverton
Newton Abbot
Dartmoor
High Willhays 621
Plymouth
Saltash
Eddystone
Exe
Teign
Dart
Tamar
Bodmin
Bodmin Moor
Brown Willy 419
St. Austell
Truro
Falmouth
Lizard
Redruth
Camborne
Penzance
Newquay
St. Ives
Land's End
Milton Keynes
Northampton
Rushden
Wellingborough
Kettering
Corby
Rugby
Coventry
Royal Leamington Spa
Warwick
Stratford-upon-Avon
Banbury
Oxford
Swindon
Cirencester
Cheltenham
Gloucester
Tewkesbury
Evesham
Redditch
Solihull
Birmingham
West Bromwich
Dudley
Sutton Coldfield
Nuneaton
Hinckley
Atherstone
Stourbridge
Kidderminster
Worcester
Great Malvern
Hereford
Ross-on-Wye
Monmouth
Newport
Cwmbran
Pontypool
Cwmbran
Cardiff
Barry
Bridgend
Port Talbot
Neath
Swansea
Llanelli
Carmarthen
Haverfordwest
Milford Haven
Pembroke
Fishguard
St. David's Head
Cardigan
Aberystwyth
Cardigan Bay
Newtown
Llandrindod Wells
Builth Wells
Brecon
Abergavenny
Merthyr Tydfil
Aberdare
Rhondda
Pontypridd
Caerphilly
Ebbw Vale
Brecon Beacons 886
Cambrian Mountains
Plynlimon Fawr 752
Snowdonia
W A L E S
Bristol
Bath
Mendip Hills
Weston-super-Mare
Bridgwater
Bridgwater Bay
Minehead
Ilfracombe
Hartland Point
Lundy
Bude
Dunkery Beacon 520
Chipenham
Trowbridge
Frome
Stonehenge
Salisbury Plain
Chiltern Hills
Cotswold Hills
Watford
Chelmsford

Bristol Channel

Cardigan Bay

52°
52°
51°
50°
50°

4°
3°
2°
1°
0°
1°

West from Greenwich   East from Greenwich

See page 15 for counties and regions

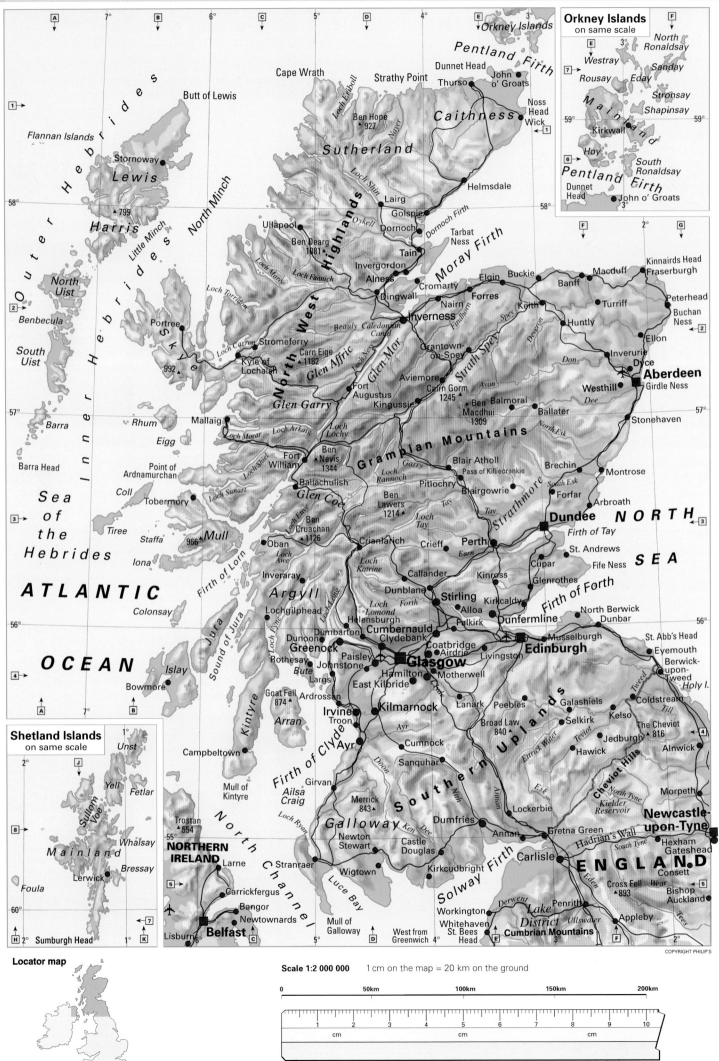

Scale 1:2 000 000   1 cm on the map = 20 km on the ground

0   50km   100km   150km   200km

Locator map

COPYRIGHT PHILIP'S

Height of the land (metres)

- over 1000
- 400-1000
- 200-400
- 100-200
- 0-100
- sea level
- below sea level

Key to map symbols

- ■ Over 1,000,000 inhabitants
- ◼ 100,000 - 1,000,000 inhabitants
- ● 50,000 - 100,000 inhabitants
- • Under 50,000 inhabitants

Dublin Capital cities underlined

Scale 1:2 000 000

- ——— Main roads
- ——— Railways
- ✈ International airports
- ⊷⊶⊷ Country boundaries

See page 15 for counties and regions

Locator map

COPYRIGHT PHILIP'S

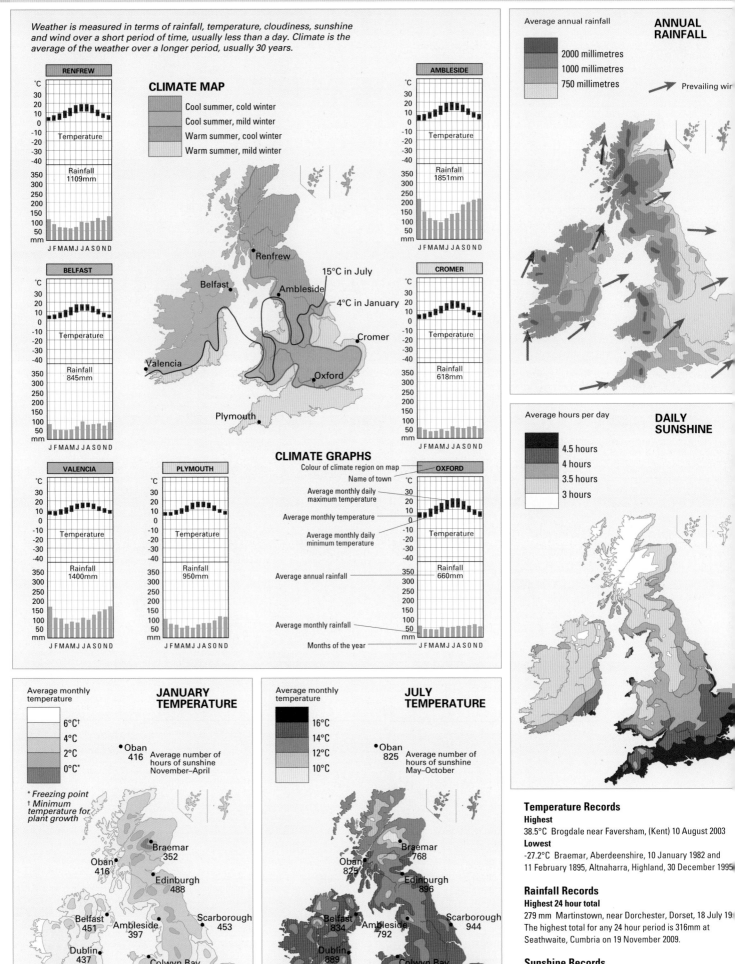

Weather is measured in terms of rainfall, temperature, cloudiness, sunshine and wind over a short period of time, usually less than a day. Climate is the average of the weather over a longer period, usually 30 years.

Temperature Records
Highest
38.5°C Brogdale near Faversham, (Kent) 10 August 2003
Lowest
-27.2°C Braemar, Aberdeenshire, 10 January 1982 and
11 February 1895, Altnaharra, Highland, 30 December 1995

Rainfall Records
Highest 24 hour total
279 mm Martinstown, near Dorchester, Dorset, 18 July 19...
The highest total for any 24 hour period is 316mm at
Seathwaite, Cumbria on 19 November 2009.

Sunshine Records
Highest monthly total
390 hours Eastbourne and Hastings, Sussex, July 1911
Lowest monthly total
0 hours Westminster, Greater London, December 1890

Winds (highest gusts)
150 knots Cairngorm, 20 March 1986

COPYRIGHT PHILIP'S

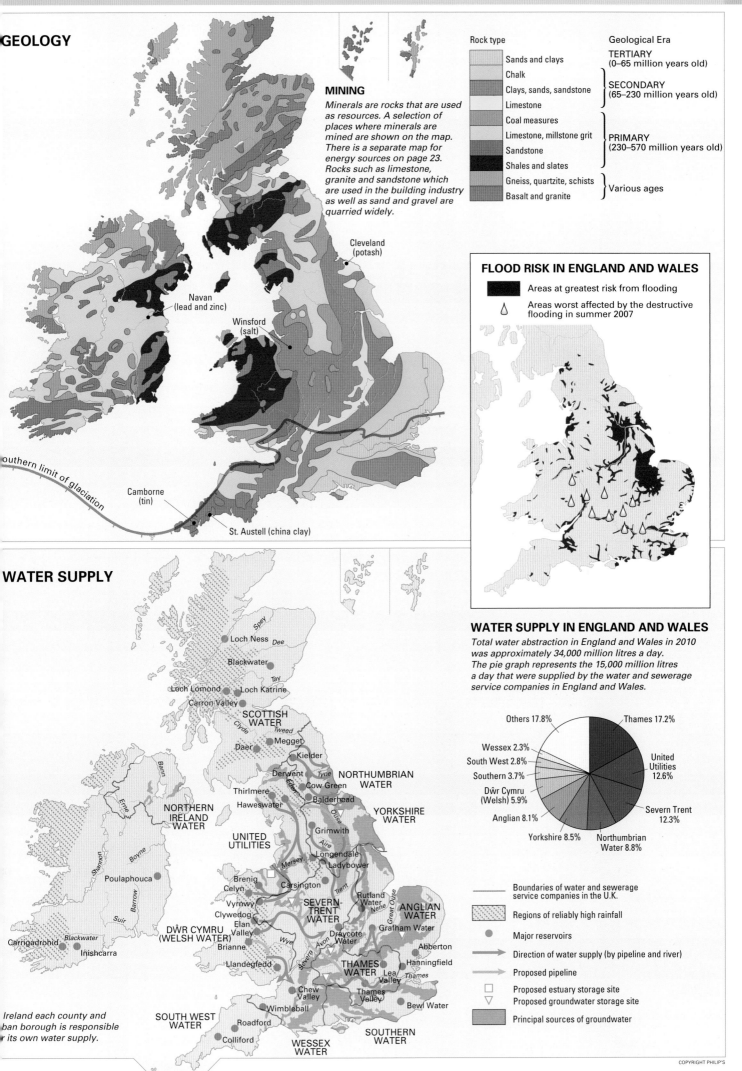

GEOLOGY

Rock type		Geological Era
	Sands and clays	TERTIARY (0–65 million years old)
	Chalk	SECONDARY (65–230 million years old)
	Clays, sands, sandstone	
	Limestone	
	Coal measures	PRIMARY (230–570 million years old)
	Limestone, millstone grit	
	Sandstone	
	Shales and slates	
	Gneiss, quartzite, schists	Various ages
	Basalt and granite	

MINING

Minerals are rocks that are used as resources. A selection of places where minerals are mined are shown on the map. There is a separate map for energy sources on page 23. Rocks such as limestone, granite and sandstone which are used in the building industry as well as sand and gravel are quarried widely.

Cleveland (potash)

Navan (lead and zinc)

Winsford (salt)

Southern limit of glaciation

Camborne (tin)

St. Austell (china clay)

FLOOD RISK IN ENGLAND AND WALES

■ Areas at greatest risk from flooding

⋀ Areas worst affected by the destructive flooding in summer 2007

WATER SUPPLY IN ENGLAND AND WALES

Total water abstraction in England and Wales in 2010 was approximately 34,000 million litres a day. The pie graph represents the 15,000 million litres a day that were supplied by the water and sewerage service companies in England and Wales.

Others 17.8%
Thames 17.2%
Wessex 2.3%
South West 2.8%
Southern 3.7%
United Utilities 12.6%
Dŵr Cymru (Welsh) 5.9%
Severn Trent 12.3%
Anglian 8.1%
Yorkshire 8.5%
Northumbrian Water 8.8%

—— Boundaries of water and sewerage service companies in the U.K.

▒ Regions of reliably high rainfall

● Major reservoirs

→ Direction of water supply (by pipeline and river)

→ Proposed pipeline

□ Proposed estuary storage site

▽ Proposed groundwater storage site

▒ Principal sources of groundwater

WATER SUPPLY

Spey
Loch Ness Dee
Blackwater
Tay
Loch Lomond Loch Katrine
Carron Valley
SCOTTISH WATER
Clyde
Tweed
Daer Megget
Kielder
Derwent Tyne NORTHUMBRIAN WATER
Thirlmere Cow Green
Haweswater Balderhead
YORKSHIRE WATER
Bann
NORTHERN IRELAND WATER
Erne
Grimwith
Aire
UNITED UTILITIES
Longendale
Mersey Ladybower
Boyne
Brenig Carsington
Celyn Trent
Poulaphouca
Vyrnwy Rutland Water ANGLIAN WATER
Barrow Clywedog Nene
SEVERN-TRENT WATER
Shannon
Elan Great Ouse
Suir Valley
DŴR CYMRU (WELSH WATER)
Brianne Grafham Water
Draycote Water
Abberton
Carrigadrohid Blackwater
Llandegfedd Avon Hanningfield
Inishcarra Wye
THAMES WATER
Lea Thames
Valley
Chew Valley Thames
Wimbleball Valley
Bewl Water
SOUTH WEST WATER
Roadford
SOUTHERN WATER
Colliford
WESSEX WATER

Ireland each county and urban borough is responsible for its own water supply.

COPYRIGHT PHILIP'S

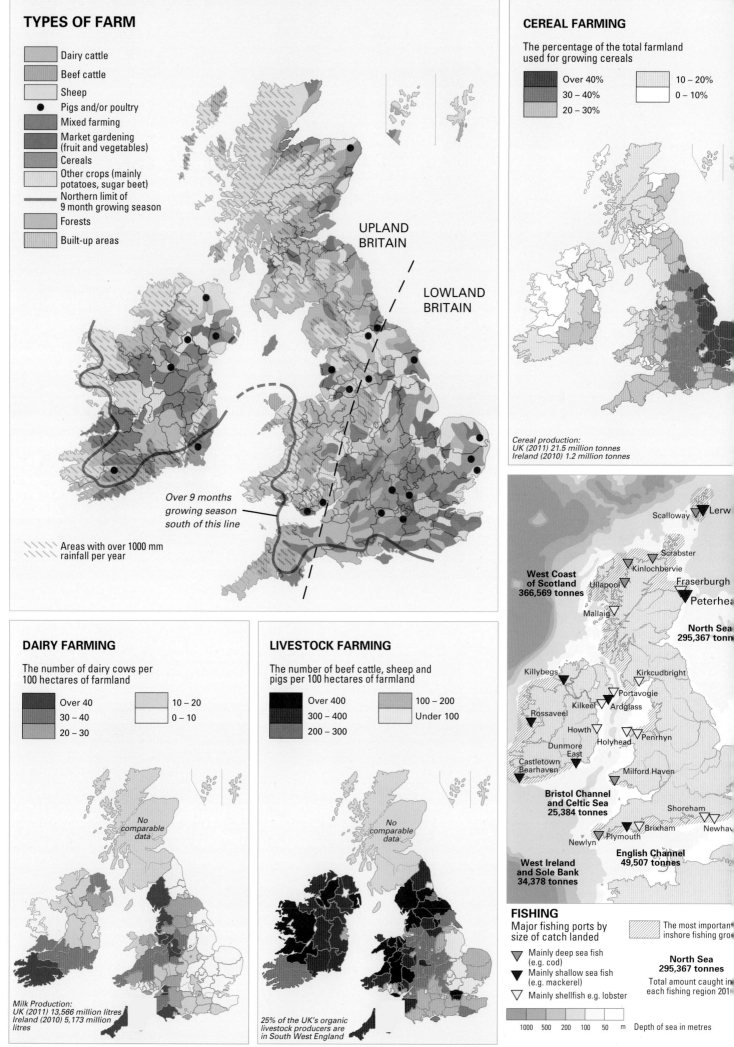

TYPES OF FARM

- Dairy cattle
- Beef cattle
- Sheep
- ● Pigs and/or poultry
- Mixed farming
- Market gardening (fruit and vegetables)
- Cereals
- Other crops (mainly potatoes, sugar beet)
- Northern limit of 9 month growing season
- Forests
- Built-up areas

UPLAND BRITAIN

LOWLAND BRITAIN

Over 9 months growing season south of this line

Areas with over 1000 mm rainfall per year

CEREAL FARMING

The percentage of the total farmland used for growing cereals

- Over 40%
- 30 – 40%
- 20 – 30%
- 10 – 20%
- 0 – 10%

Cereal production:
UK (2011) 21.5 million tonnes
Ireland (2010) 1.2 million tonnes

DAIRY FARMING

The number of dairy cows per 100 hectares of farmland

- Over 40
- 30 – 40
- 20 – 30
- 10 – 20
- 0 – 10

No comparable data

Milk Production:
UK (2011) 13,566 million litres
Ireland (2010) 5,173 million litres

LIVESTOCK FARMING

The number of beef cattle, sheep and pigs per 100 hectares of farmland

- Over 400
- 300 – 400
- 200 – 300
- 100 – 200
- Under 100

No comparable data

25% of the UK's organic livestock producers are in South West England

FISHING

Major fishing ports by size of catch landed

- ▽ Mainly deep sea fish (e.g. cod)
- ▼ Mainly shallow sea fish (e.g. mackerel)
- ▽ Mainly shellfish e.g. lobster

The most important inshore fishing ground

North Sea 295,367 tonnes
Total amount caught in each fishing region 201

1000 500 200 100 50 m Depth of sea in metres

Scalloway Lerw

Scrabster
Kinlochbervie
West Coast of Scotland 366,569 tonnes Ullapool Fraserburgh Peterhea

Mallaig

North Sea 295,367 tonn

Killybegs Kirkcudbright
Portavogie
Kilkeel Ardglass
Rossaveel Howth Holyhead Penrhyn
Dunmore East
Castletown Bearhaven Milford Haven
Bristol Channel and Celtic Sea 25,384 tonnes Shoreham
Newlyn Brixham Newha
Plymouth
English Channel 49,507 tonnes
West Ireland and Sole Bank 34,378 tonnes

COPYRIGHT PHILIP'S

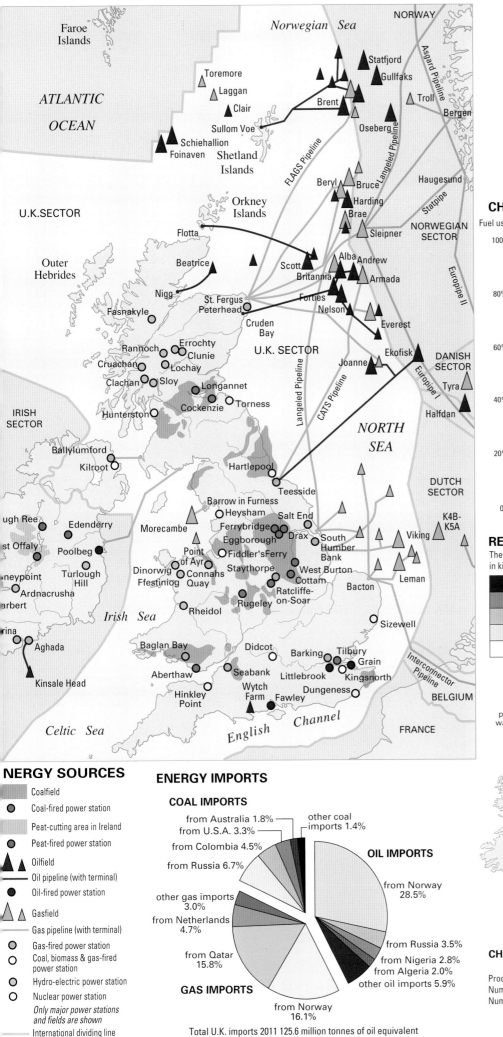

Map labels:

Faroe Islands
Norwegian Sea
NORWAY
ATLANTIC OCEAN
Toremore
Laggan
Clair
Statfjord
Gullfaks
Brent
Troll
Bergen
Sullom Voe
Schiehallion
Foinaven
Shetland Islands
Oseberg
Asgard Pipeline
FLAGS Pipeline
Langeled Pipeline
Haugesund
Beryl
Bruce
Harding
Brae
Sleipner
Statpipe
NORWEGIAN SECTOR
U.K. SECTOR
Orkney Islands
Flotta
Beatrice
Scott
Britannia
Alba
Andrew
Armada
Forties
Nelson
Nigg
St. Fergus
Peterhead
Cruden Bay
Everest
Ekofisk
Joanne
Europipe II
DANISH SECTOR
Tyra
Halfdan
Outer Hebrides
Fasnakyle
Rannoch
Errochty
Clunie
Cruachan
Lochay
Clachan
Sloy
Longannet
Cockenzie
Torness
Hunterston
U.K. SECTOR
Langeled Pipeline
CATS Pipeline
NORTH SEA
DUTCH SECTOR
K4B-K5A
IRISH SECTOR
Ballylumford
Kilroot
Hartlepool
Teesside
Viking
Leman
ugh Ree
Edenderry
st Offaly
Poolbeg
neypoint
Turlough Hill
Ardnacrusha
arbert
rina
Aghada
Kinsale Head
Morecambe
Barrow in Furness
Heysham
Ferrybridge
Eggborough
Fiddler's Ferry
Point of Ayr
Dinorwig
Connahs Quay
Ffestiniog
Staythorpe
Rugeley
Ratcliffe-on-Soar
Rheidol
Salt End
Drax
South Humber Bank
West Burton
Cottam
Bacton
Baglan Bay
Aberthaw
Didcot
Seabank
Hinkley Point
Wytch Farm
Fawley
Barking
Littlebrook
Tilbury
Grain
Kingsnorth
Dungeness
Sizewell
Interconnector Pipeline
BELGIUM
Irish Sea
Celtic Sea
English Channel
FRANCE

COPYRIGHT PHILIP'S

ENERGY CONSUMPTION BY FUEL

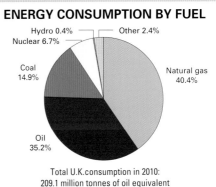

Hydro 0.4%
Nuclear 6.7%
Other 2.4%
Coal 14.9%
Natural gas 40.4%
Oil 35.2%

Total U.K. consumption in 2010:
209.1 million tonnes of oil equivalent

CHANGES IN ELECTRICITY GENERATION

Fuel used in the generation of electricity in the U.K. 1980 – 2010

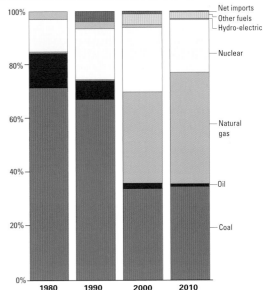

Net imports
Other fuels
Hydro-electric
Nuclear
Natural gas
Oil
Coal

100% 80% 60% 40% 20% 0%
1980 1990 2000 2010

RENEWABLE ENERGY

The amount of energy generated from renewable sources in kilowatt hours, 2010

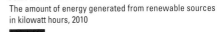

30,000
20,000
10,000
5,000

Major wind farm
Possible sites for tidal power generation

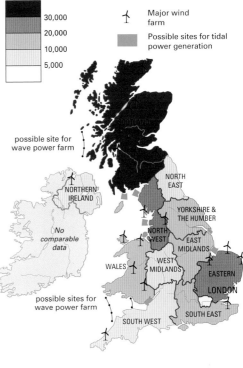

possible site for wave power farm
NORTHERN IRELAND
No comparable data
NORTH EAST
YORKSHIRE & THE HUMBER
NORTH WEST
EAST MIDLANDS
WALES
WEST MIDLANDS
EASTERN
LONDON
SOUTH WEST
SOUTH EAST
possible sites for wave power farm

CHANGES TO COAL MINING IN THE U.K.

	1960	1980	2010
Production (million tonnes)	195	126	18
Number of employees (thousands)	631	297	9
Number of deep mines	698	211	12

NERGY SOURCES

- Coalfield
- Coal-fired power station
- Peat-cutting area in Ireland
- Peat-fired power station
- ▲ Oilfield
- — Oil pipeline (with terminal)
- ● Oil-fired power station
- ▲ Gasfield
- — Gas pipeline (with terminal)
- Gas-fired power station
- Coal, biomass & gas-fired power station
- Hydro-electric power station
- Nuclear power station
- *Only major power stations and fields are shown*
- — International dividing line

ENERGY IMPORTS

COAL IMPORTS

from Australia 1.8%
from U.S.A. 3.3%
from Colombia 4.5%
from Russia 6.7%
other coal imports 1.4%

OIL IMPORTS

from Norway 28.5%
from Russia 3.5%
from Nigeria 2.8%
from Algeria 2.0%
other oil imports 5.9%

other gas imports 3.0%
from Netherlands 4.7%
from Qatar 15.8%

GAS IMPORTS

from Norway 16.1%

Total U.K. imports 2011 125.6 million tonnes of oil equivalent

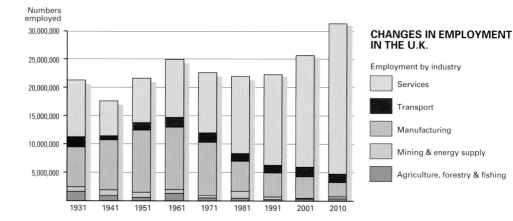

Numbers employed

CHANGES IN EMPLOYMENT IN THE U.K.

Employment by industry

- Services
- Transport
- Manufacturing
- Mining & energy supply
- Agriculture, forestry & fishing

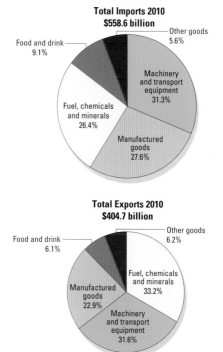

▲ Canary Wharf, London, is a centre of banking - important part of the service industry.

▲ These Mini Clubman cars are being manufactured at the BMW factory, Oxford.

▲ An engineer is shown working on a jet engine in the Rolls-Royce factory, Derby.

INCOME

The average gross weekly earnings of males and females in full employment in 2010

Over £600	£450 – £500
£550 – £600	£400 – £450
£500 – £550	Under £400

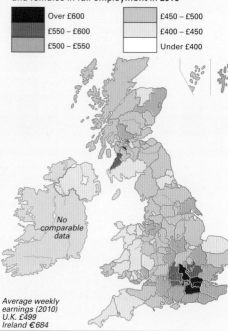

No comparable data

Average weekly earnings (2010)
U.K. £499
Ireland €684

EMPLOYMENT IN SERVICES

The percentage of the workforce employed in the service industry in 2010

Over 85%	70 – 75%
80 – 85%	Under 70%
75 – 80%	

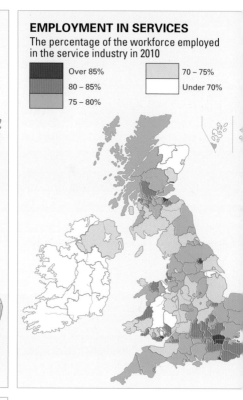

EMPLOYMENT IN MANUFACTURING INDUSTRY

The percentage of the workforce employed in manufacturing in 2010

Over 20%	12% – 14%
16% – 20%	10% – 12%
14% – 16%	Under 10%

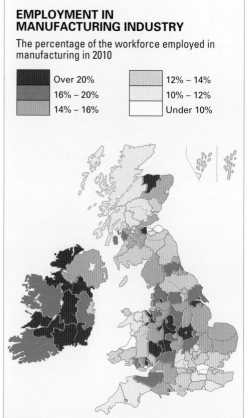

UNEMPLOYMENT

The percentage of the workforce unemployed in 2010

Over 12%	6% – 8%
10% – 12%	4% – 6%
8% – 10%	Under 4%

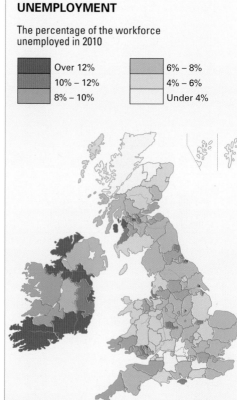

U.K. TRADE

Trade is balanced by money coming in for service such as banking and insurance.

Total Imports 2010
$558.6 billion

- Food and drink 9.1%
- Other goods 5.6%
- Machinery and transport equipment 31.3%
- Fuel, chemicals and minerals 26.4%
- Manufactured goods 27.6%

Total Exports 2010
$404.7 billion

- Food and drink 6.1%
- Other goods 6.2%
- Fuel, chemicals and minerals 33.2%
- Manufactured goods 22.9%
- Machinery and transport equipment 31.6%

COPYRIGHT PHILIP'S

POPULATION FACTS

U.K. Population 2012	**63,047,000**
of which England	52,921,000
Scotland	5,255,000
Wales	3,060,000
Northern Ireland	1,811,000
Ireland Population 2012	**4,722,000**

AGE STRUCTURE OF THE U.K. IN 1901 AND 2010

The age structure shows how old people are and the percentage in each age group that is male and female. Each diagram is called a population pyramid. For example, in 1901, 20% of the female population was aged between 0–19. In 2010, about 12% were in this group.

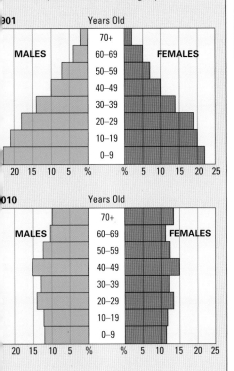

1901 — Years Old
MALES / FEMALES
70+, 60–69, 50–59, 40–49, 30–39, 20–29, 10–19, 0–9
20 15 10 5 % % 5 10 15 20 25

2010 — Years Old
MALES / FEMALES
70+, 60–69, 50–59, 40–49, 30–39, 20–29, 10–19, 0–9
20 15 10 5 % % 5 10 15 20 25

POPULATION DENSITY

Number of people per square kilometre in 2011

- Over 1000
- 500 – 1000
- 200 – 500
- 100 – 200
- 50 – 100
- 25 – 50
- Under 25

The average density for the U.K. is 261 people per km².

The average density for Ireland is 67 people per km².

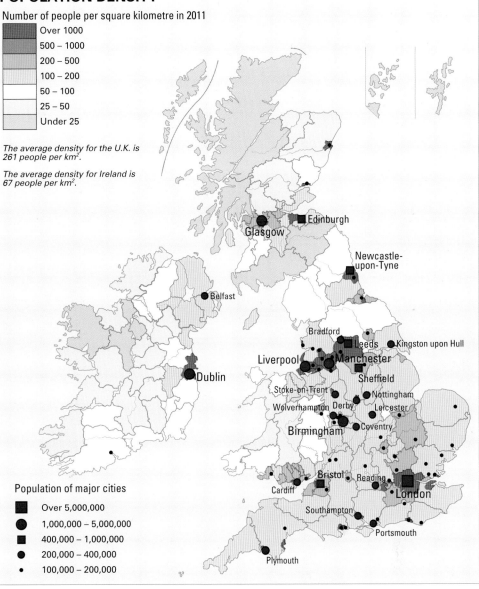

Population of major cities
- ■ Over 5,000,000
- ● 1,000,000 – 5,000,000
- ■ 400,000 – 1,000,000
- ● 200,000 – 400,000
- • 100,000 – 200,000

Cities labelled: Glasgow, Edinburgh, Newcastle-upon-Tyne, Belfast, Bradford, Leeds, Kingston upon Hull, Liverpool, Manchester, Dublin, Sheffield, Stoke-on-Trent, Nottingham, Wolverhampton, Derby, Leicester, Birmingham, Coventry, Bristol, Reading, Cardiff, London, Southampton, Portsmouth, Plymouth

ETHNIC GROUPS

Ethnic minorities as a % of total population in 2010

- Over 25%
- 10 – 25%
- 5 – 10%
- 0 – 5%

Ethnic minority groups

38 000 Total number of ethnic minority people in each region

SCOTLAND 135 000
NORTH EAST 138 000
YORKSHIRE & THE HUMBER 545 000
NORTH WEST & MERSEYSIDE 575 000
EAST MIDLANDS 440 000
WEST MIDLANDS 760 000
EAST 575 000
WALES 124 000
No comparable data
LONDON 2 348 000
SOUTH WEST 311 000
SOUTH EAST 785 000

% foreign born by country;
U.K. (excl. N.Ireland) 10.4%
Ireland 19.6%

YOUNG PEOPLE

The percentage of the population under 15 years old in 2010

- Over 22%
- 20 – 22%
- 18 – 20%
- 16 – 18%
- 14 – 16%

% young by country
U.K. 18.6%
Ireland 21.5%

OLD PEOPLE

The percentage of the population over pensionable age in 2010

- Over 22%
- 20 – 22%
- 18 – 20%
- 16 – 18%
- 14 – 16%
- Under 14%

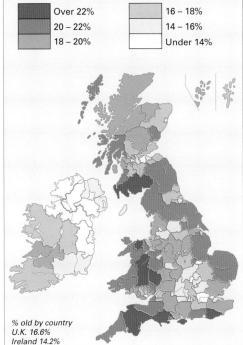

% old by country
U.K. 16.6%
Ireland 14.2%

COPYRIGHT PHILIP'S

ROADS AND FERRIES

- M6 Motorways
- Other main roads
- Principal car ferry routes

Scrabster • Stornoway • Wick • Kirkwall • Lerwick • Ullapool • Invergordon • Inverness • Aberdeen • Oban • Perth • Dundee • Glasgow • Troon • Edinburgh M8 • Derry/Londonderry • Larne • Stranraer • Carlisle • Newcastle • Belfast • Sligo • Dundalk • Morecambe • Douglas • Fleetwood • Leeds • Hull • Liverpool • Manchester • Sheffield • Galway • Dublin • Holyhead • Shrewsbury • Leicester • Norwich • Dún Laoghaire • Limerick • Waterford • Rosslare • Birmingham • Cambridge • Harwich Felixstowe • Killarney • Cork • Fishguard • Pembroke • Swansea • Oxford • London • Ramsgate • Cardiff • Bristol • Dunkirk • Exeter • Southampton • Portsmouth • Dover • Calais • Plymouth • Weymouth • Poole • Newhaven • Boulogne • Penzance

RAILWAYS

- Electrified lines
- Other main lines
- High-speed rail link
- Planned high-speed rail link (HS2)

The fastest journey time from London to Paris via the Channel Tunnel is now 2 hours 15 minutes, London to Brussels is 1 hour 51 minutes.

Inverness • Aberdeen • Perth • Dundee • Stirling • Gourock • Glasgow • Edinburgh • Portrush • Kilmarnock • Derry/Londonderry • Larne • Dumfries • Carlisle • Newcastle • Sunderland • Ballina • Sligo • Belfast • Darlington • Westport • Dundalk • Barrow • York • Hull • Athlone • Mullingar • Blackpool • Leeds • Grimsby • Galway • Dublin • Preston • Manchester • Doncaster • Liverpool • Sheffield • Nottingham • Kilkenny • Holyhead • Crewe • Derby • King's Lynn • Limerick • Shrewsbury • Birmingham • Leicester • Tralee • Worcester • Rugby • Peterborough • Waterford • Rosslare • Hereford • Northampton • Cambridge • Cork • Fishguard • Gloucester • Oxford • Swindon • London • Swansea • Cardiff • Reading • Taunton • Bath • Southampton • Folkestone • Bournemouth • Hastings • Exeter • Brighton • Eastbourne • Penzance • Weymouth • Plymouth • Portsmouth

AIRPORTS

Passenger traffic in thousands (2010)

60,000 / 30,000 / 5,000 / 1,000

Stornoway • Kirkwall • Seatsta • Sumburgh • Inverness • Aberdeen • Glasgow International • Edinburgh • City of Derry • Glasgow Prestwick • Newcastle • Belfast International • George Best Belfast City • Durham Tees Valley • Isle of Man • Leeds/Bradford International • Ireland West (Knock) • Blackpool • Robin Hood Doncaster/Sheffield • Liverpool John Lennon • Galway • Dublin • Humberside • Manchester • East Midlands • Shannon • Norwich International • Kerry • Birmingham • Cork • Waterford • London Luton • Bristol International • Cardiff • London Stansted • Exeter International • London Heathrow • London City • Newquay • Bournemouth • London Gatwick • Isles of Scilly • Southampton

SEAPORTS

Goods traffic by port in thousand tonnes (2010)

50,000 / 25,000 / 10,000 / 5,000

Orkney • Sullom Voe • Cromarty Firth • Aberdeen • Glensanda (Aggregates) • Forth • Clyde • Larne • Tyne • Tees & Hartlepool • Belfast • Heysham • Humber • Warrenpoint • Liverpool • Goole • Hull • All Irish Ports • Dublin • Holyhead • Manchester • Grimsby & Immingham • Dún Laoghaire • Shannon Foynes • Waterford • Rosslare • Felixstowe • Cork • Newport • London • Ipswich • Milford Haven • Bristol • Port Talbot • Cardiff • Dover • Medway • Plymouth • Portsmouth • Southampton

TOURIST TRAFFIC

Millions of visitors from U.K. (2010)

0 1 2 3 4 5 6 7 8 9 10

Spain	
France	
U.S.A.	
Ireland	
Italy	
Germany	
Portugal	
Turkey	
Netherlands	
Greece	

VISITS ABROAD BY U.K. RESIDENTS

VISITS TO U.K. BY FOREIGN VISITORS

Italy
Netherlands
Spain
Ireland
U.S.A.
Germany
France

4 3 2 1 0
Millions of visitors to the U.K. (2010)

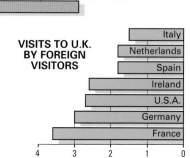

▲ Eurostar at St. Pancras International. This station is the London terminus of the high-speed rail link to Europe, High Speed 1.

COPYRIGHT PHILIP'S

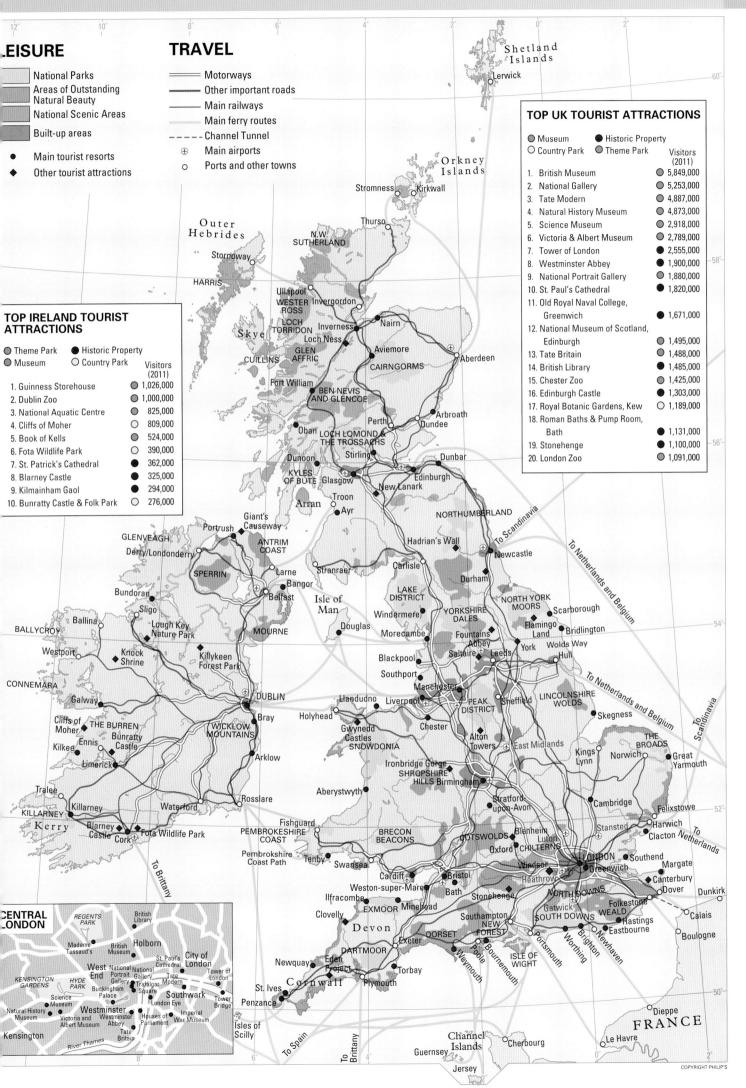

LEISURE

- National Parks
- Areas of Outstanding Natural Beauty
- National Scenic Areas
- Built-up areas
- Main tourist resorts
- Other tourist attractions

TRAVEL

- Motorways
- Other important roads
- Main railways
- Main ferry routes
- Channel Tunnel
- Main airports
- Ports and other towns

TOP UK TOURIST ATTRACTIONS

- Museum
- Country Park
- Historic Property
- Theme Park

		Visitors (2011)
1.	British Museum	5,849,000
2.	National Gallery	5,253,000
3.	Tate Modern	4,887,000
4.	Natural History Museum	4,873,000
5.	Science Museum	2,918,000
6.	Victoria & Albert Museum	2,789,000
7.	Tower of London	2,555,000
8.	Westminster Abbey	1,900,000
9.	National Portrait Gallery	1,880,000
10.	St. Paul's Cathedral	1,820,000
11.	Old Royal Naval College, Greenwich	1,671,000
12.	National Museum of Scotland, Edinburgh	1,495,000
13.	Tate Britain	1,488,000
14.	British Library	1,485,000
15.	Chester Zoo	1,425,000
16.	Edinburgh Castle	1,303,000
17.	Royal Botanic Gardens, Kew	1,189,000
18.	Roman Baths & Pump Room, Bath	1,131,000
19.	Stonehenge	1,100,000
20.	London Zoo	1,091,000

TOP IRELAND TOURIST ATTRACTIONS

- Theme Park
- Museum
- Historic Property
- Country Park

		Visitors (2011)
1.	Guinness Storehouse	1,026,000
2.	Dublin Zoo	1,000,000
3.	National Aquatic Centre	825,000
4.	Cliffs of Moher	809,000
5.	Book of Kells	524,000
6.	Fota Wildlife Park	390,000
7.	St. Patrick's Cathedral	362,000
8.	Blarney Castle	325,000
9.	Kilmainham Gaol	294,000
10.	Bunratty Castle & Folk Park	276,000

CENTRAL LONDON

Regents Park
British Library
Madame Tussaud's
British Museum
Holborn
St. Paul's Cathedral
City of London
West End
National Portrait Gallery
National Gallery
Tate Modern
Tower of London
KENSINGTON GARDENS
HYDE PARK
Trafalgar Square
Buckingham Palace
Science Museum
Southwark
London Eye
Tower Bridge
Natural History Museum
Westminster
Victoria and Albert Museum
Westminster Abbey
Houses of Parliament
Imperial War Museum
Tate Britain
Kensington
River Thames

COPYRIGHT PHILIP'S

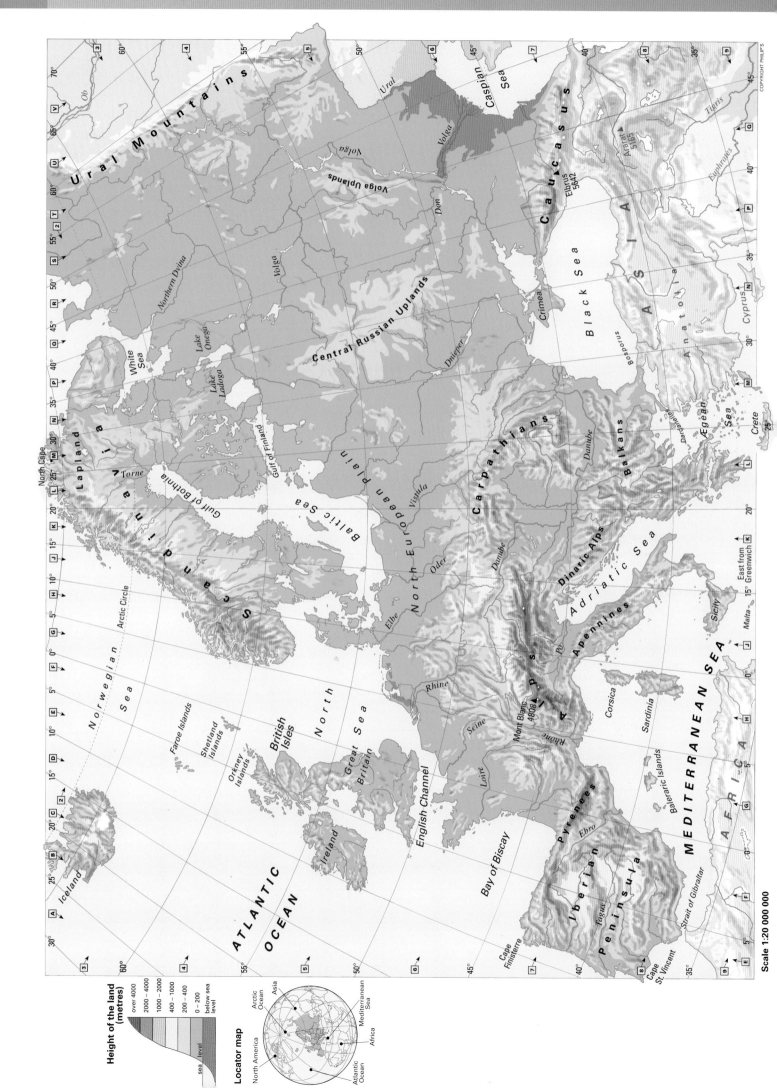

COPYRIGHT PHILIP'S

Height of the land (metres)

over 4000
2000 – 4000
1000 – 2000
400 – 1000
200 – 400
0 – 200
below sea level

sea level

Locator map

Arctic Ocean
Asia
North America
Atlantic Ocean
Mediterranean Sea
Africa

Scale 1:20 000 000

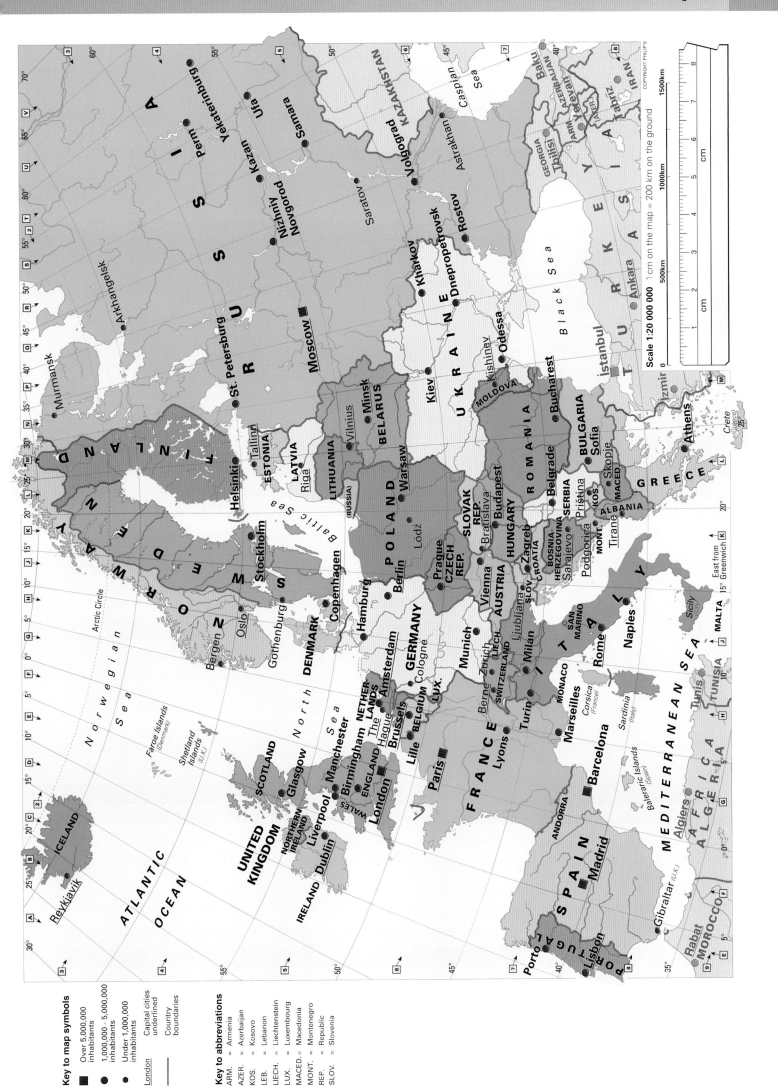

Key to map symbols

- ■ Over 5,000,000 inhabitants
- ● 1,000,000 – 5,000,000 inhabitants
- • Under 1,000,000 inhabitants
- London Capital cities underlined
- Country boundaries

Key to abbreviations

ARM. = Armenia
AZER. = Azerbaijan
KOS. = Kosovo
LEB. = Lebanon
LIECH. = Liechtenstein
LUX. = Luxembourg
MACED. = Macedonia
MONT. = Montenegro
REP. = Republic
SLOV. = Slovenia

Scale 1:20 000 000

1 cm on the map = 200 km on the ground

COPYRIGHT PHILIP'S

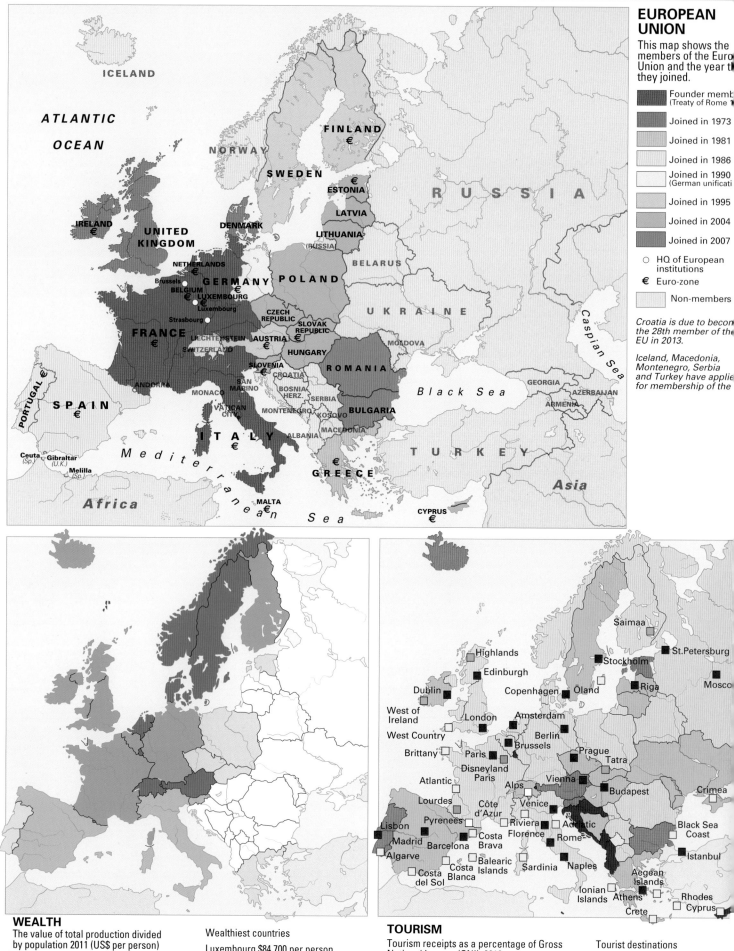

ICELAND

ATLANTIC OCEAN

NORWAY

SWEDEN

FINLAND €

ESTONIA

LATVIA

LITHUANIA (RUSSIA)

RUSSIA

BELARUS

UKRAINE

IRELAND €

UNITED KINGDOM

DENMARK

NETHERLANDS

Brussels
GERMANY €
BELGIUM €
LUXEMBOURG €
Luxembourg

POLAND

CZECH REPUBLIC

Strasbourg

FRANCE €

LIECHTENSTEIN
SWITZERLAND

SLOVAK REPUBLIC

AUSTRIA €

HUNGARY

MOLDOVA

SLOVENIA

ANDORRA

MONACO

SAN MARINO

CROATIA

BOSNIA HERZ.

SERBIA

ROMANIA

Caspian Sea

GEORGIA

AZERBAIJAN

ARMENIA

Black Sea

PORTUGAL €

SPAIN €

VATICAN CITY

ITALY €

MONTENEGRO
KOSOVO
MACEDONIA
ALBANIA

BULGARIA

Ceuta (Sp.) Gibraltar (U.K.)
Melilla (Sp.)

Mediterranean Sea

GREECE €

TURKEY

Asia

Africa

MALTA €

CYPRUS €

EUROPEAN UNION

This map shows the members of the European Union and the year that they joined.

Founder members (Treaty of Rome 1)

Joined in 1973

Joined in 1981

Joined in 1986

Joined in 1990 (German unification)

Joined in 1995

Joined in 2004

Joined in 2007

○ HQ of European institutions

€ Euro-zone

Non-members

Croatia is due to become the 28th member of the EU in 2013.

Iceland, Macedonia, Montenegro, Serbia and Turkey have applied for membership of the

Highlands
Edinburgh
Dublin
West of Ireland
West Country
Brittany
Atlantic
Lourdes
Lisbon
Madrid
Algarve
Costa del Sol
London
Paris
Disneyland Paris
Pyrenees
Barcelona
Costa Blanca
Balearic Islands
Amsterdam
Brussels
Alps
Côte d'Azur
Costa Brava
Sardinia
Copenhagen
Öland
Berlin
Vienna
Venice
Riviera
Florence
Naples
Stockholm
Prague
Tatra
Budapest
Adriatic
Rome
Saimaa
St.Petersburg
Riga
Moscow
Crimea
Black Sea Coast
Istanbul
Aegean Islands
Ionian Islands
Athens
Crete
Rhodes
Cyprus

WEALTH

The value of total production divided by population 2011 (US$ per person)

Over $40,000 per person

$35,000 – 40,000 per person

$30,000 – 35,000 per person

$20,000 – 30,000 per person

Under $ 20,000 per person

UK $35,900 per person

Wealthiest countries

Luxembourg $84,700 per person
Norway $53,300 per person
Switzerland $43,400 per person

Poorest countries

Ukraine $7,200 per person
Kosovo $6,500 per person
Moldova $3,400 per person

TOURISM

Tourism receipts as a percentage of Gross National Income (GNI), 2010

Over 10% of GNI from tourism

5–10% of GNI from tourism

2.5–5% of GNI from tourism

Under 2.5% of GNI from tourism

Tourist destinations

■ Cultural & historical centres

☐ Coastal resorts

☐ Ski resorts

◼ Centres of entertainment

◼ Places of pilgrimage

◼ Places of great natural beauty

COPYRIGHT PHILIP'S

Scale 1:10 000 000   1cm on the map = 100 km on the ground

0   100km   200km   300km   400km   500km   600km

Height of the land (metres)

over 4000
2000-4000
1000-2000
400-1000
200-400
0-200
sea level
below sea level

Key to map symbols

■ Over 5,000,000 inhabitants

● 1,000,000 - 5,000,000 inhabitants

• Under 1,000,000 inhabitants

Helsinki   Capital cities underlined

— Country boundaries

Locator map

COPYRIGHT PHILIP'S

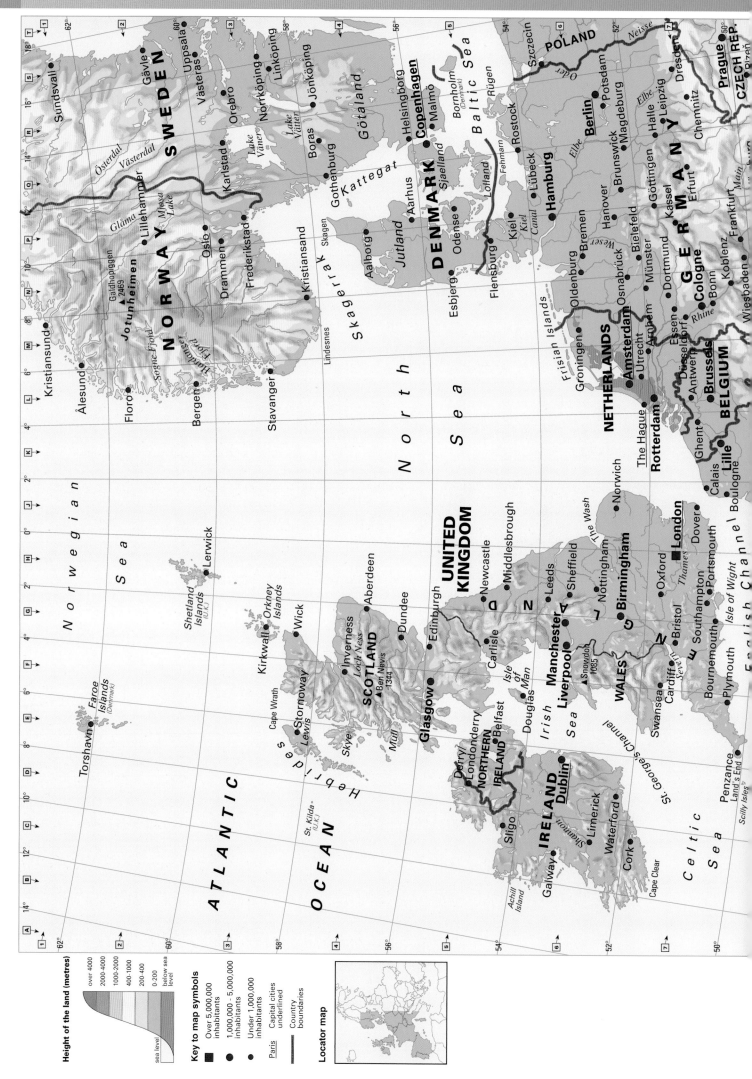

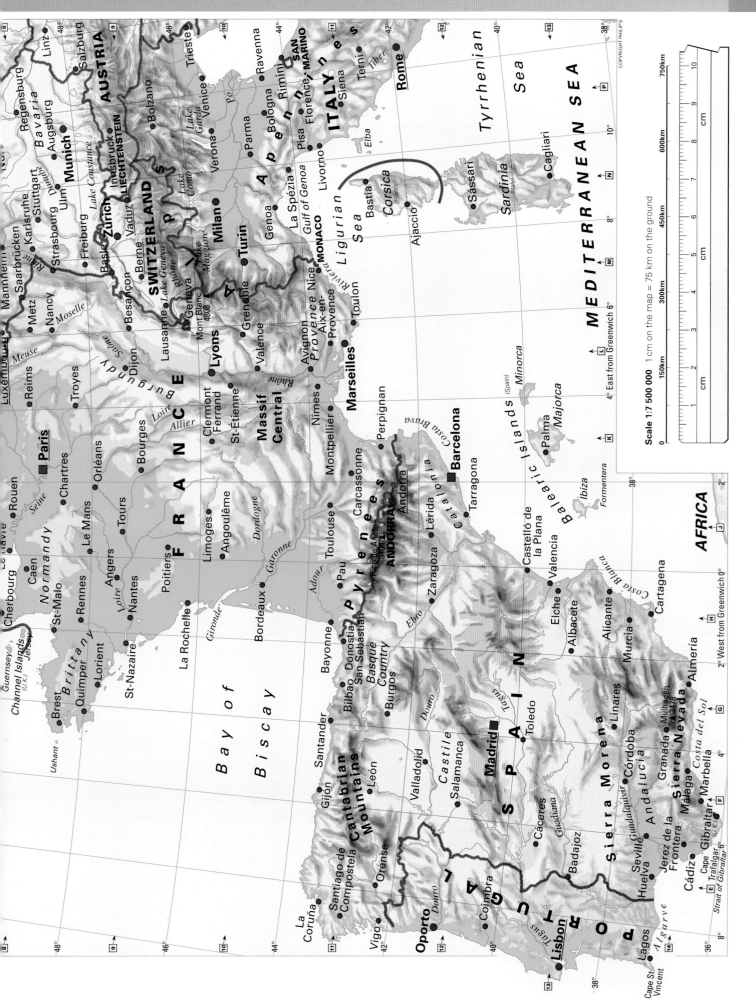

COPYRIGHT PHILIP'S

Scale 1:7 500 000 1 cm on the map = 75 km on the ground

150km 300km 450km 600km 750km

0 cm 1 2 3 4 5 6 7 8 9 10 cm

4° East from Greenwich 6° 8° 10°

2° West from Greenwich 0° 2°

AUSTRIA

Linz
Salzburg
Regensburg
Bavaria
Augsburg
Munich
Ulm
Stuttgart
Innsbruck
Salzbourg
LIECHTENSTEIN
Vaduz
Bolzano
Trieste
Venice
Lake Garda
Ravenna
Verona
Parma
Bologna
Rimini
SAN MARINO
Florence
ITALY
Siena
Terni
Tiber
Rome

Mannheim
Saarbrücken
Karlsruhe
Freiburg
Basle
Zurich
Berne
SWITZERLAND
Lake Constance
Lake Geneva
Lake Maggiore
Lake Como
Milan
Turin
Genoa
La Spézia
Gulf of Genoa
Livorno
Pisa
Apennines
Elba

Metz
Nancy
Strasbourg
Rhine
Besançon
Dijon
Lausanne
Geneva
Mont Blanc 4808
Grenoble
Lyons
Valence
Rhône
Nice
Aix-en-Provence
MONACO
Riviera
Provence
Avignon
Ligurian Sea
Bastia
Corsica (France)
Ajaccio
Sassari
Sardinia (Italy)
Cagliari

Tyrrhenian Sea

MEDITERRANEAN SEA

Luxembourg
Reims
Troyes
Meuse
Moselle
Burgundy
Saône
Allier
Loire
Clermont Ferrand
St-Étienne
Massif Central
Nîmes
Montpellier
Marseilles
Toulon
Perpignan

Paris
Chartres
Orléans
Bourges
FRANCE
Limoges
Angoulême
Dordogne
Carcassonne
Toulouse
Pyrenees
Andorra
ANDORRA
Pico de Aneto 3404
Lérida
Catalonia
Costa Brava
Barcelona
Tarragona

Rouen
Le Havre
Caen
Normandy
Le Mans
Angers
Tours
Poitiers
Loire
Nantes
St-Nazaire
La Rochelle
Bordeaux
Garonne
Gironde
Adour
Pau
Bayonne
Basque Country
San Sebastián
Donostia
Bilbao
Zaragoza
Ebro
Castelló de la Plana
Valencia
Costa Blanca
Alicante
Elche
Albacete
Murcia
Cartagena

Cherbourg
Channel Islands (U.K.)
Guernsey
Jersey
Brittany
Brest
Quimper
Lorient
St-Malo
Rennes

Bay of Biscay

Santander
Gijón
Cantabrian Mountains
León
Burgos
Valladolid
Castile
Salamanca
Douro
SPAIN
Madrid
Toledo
Tagus
Cáceres
Badajoz
Guadiana
Sierra Morena
Linares
Córdoba
Granada
Sierra Nevada
Mulhacén 3478
Costa del Sol
Almería
Guadalquivir
Seville
Andalucía
Málaga
Marbella
Gibraltar (U.K.)
Cape Trafalgar
Strait of Gibraltar

La Coruña
Santiago de Compostela
Orense
Vigo
Oporto
Douro
Coimbra
PORTUGAL
Tagus
Lisbon
Algarve
Lagos
Cape St. Vincent
Cádiz
Huelva
Jerez de la Frontera

AFRICA

Balearic Islands (Spain)
Minorca
Majorca
Palma
Ibiza
Formentera

Ushant

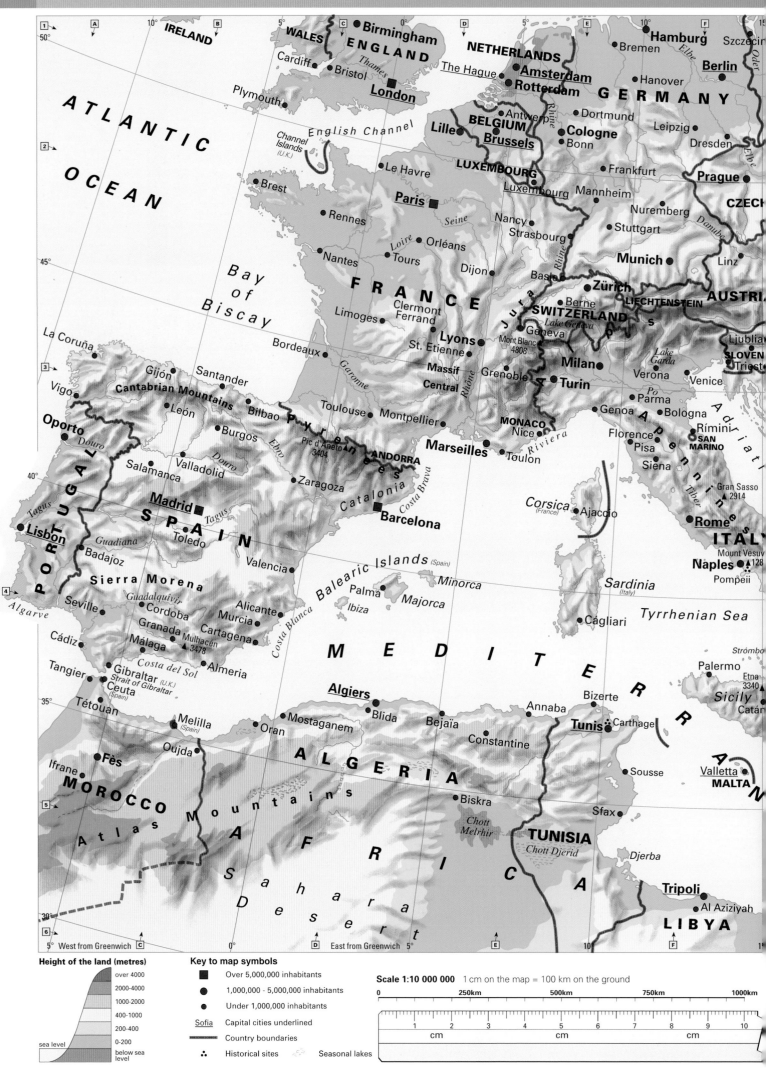

ATLANTIC

OCEAN

IRELAND

WALES

• Birmingham

ENGLAND

• Cardiff
• Bristol

• Plymouth

Thames

London

NETHERLANDS

The Hague
Amsterdam
Rotterdam

Antwerp •

Lille •

BELGIUM

Brussels

• Dortmund
• Cologne
• Bonn

Rhine

• Hamburg
Szczecin
• Bremen

• Hanover

GERMANY

Berlin

Elbe

Oder

LUXEMBOURG

Luxembourg

• Frankfurt

• Mannheim

• Leipzig
• Dresden

• Nuremberg

Prague

CZECH

Channel
Islands
(U.K.)

English Channel

• Brest

• Rennes

Paris

Seine

• Le Havre

• Nancy
• Strasbourg

Rhine

• Stuttgart

Danube

• Linz

AUSTRI

• Nantes

Loire

• Orléans
• Tours

• Dijon

FRANCE

• Basle

Zürich

SWITZERLAND

• Berne

LIECHTENSTEIN

Bay
of
Biscay

• Limoges

• Clermont
Ferrand

Massif

Central

Lyons •

St. Etienne

Jura

Mont Blanc
4808

Rhône

Geneva •

Lake Geneva

_A_

• Grenoble

Milan •

• Verona

Ljublja

SLOVEN
Trieste

• La Coruña

• Vigo

• Gijón

• Santander

Cantabrian Mountains

• León

Douro

• Burgos

Bilbao •

Pyrenees

Garonne

• Bordeaux

• Toulouse

• Montpellier

• Marseilles

Turin •

_Po_

• Parma

Genoa •

Riviera

Nice •

Toulon •

MONACO

_Lake
Garda_

• Venice

Apennin

• Bologna

• Florence

• Pisa

• Siena

Rímini •

SAN
MARINO

Adriati

Oporto

PORTUGAL

Douro

• Salamanca

• Valladolid

SPAIN

Madrid

• Toledo

Tagus

Ebro

Pic d'Aneto
3404

Zaragoza •

ANDORRA

Catalonia

Costa Brava

Barcelona

Corsica
(France)

• Ajaccio

Gran Sasso
▲ 2914

Rome

ITAL

Tagus

Guadiana

Lisbon

• Badajoz

Sierra Morena

Guadalquivir

• Córdoba

• Granada
Mulhacén
▲ 3478

• Valencia

Costa Blanca

Balearic Islands (Spain)

• Palma
• Ibiza

Minorca

• Majorca

Sardinia
(Italy)

Mount Vesuv
▲ 128

Naples

Pompeii

Tyrrhenian Sea

Strómbo

ITALY

• Alicante
• Murcia
• Cartagena

Algarve

• Seville

• Málaga

• Almería

Costa del Sol

• Cádiz

• Tangier

Gibraltar (U.K.)
Strait of Gibraltar
Ceuta
(Spain)

• Tétouan

Melilla
(Spain)

• Oran

• Mostaganem

Algiers

• Blida

MEDITERR

• Bejaïa

• Annaba

• Bizerte

Tunis

Carthage

R

Palermo •

Etna
3340 ▲

Sicily

Catár

• Ifrane

• Fès

MOROCCO

Oujda •

Atlas   Mountains

_A_

_S_

ALGERIA

• Constantine

• Biskra

_Chott
Melrhir_

TUNISIA

Chott Djerid

• Sousse

• Sfax

A
N

Valletta

MALTA

Sahara   Desert

• Djerba

• Tripoli

• Al Aziziyah

LIBYA

West from Greenwich

East from Greenwich

Height of the land (metres)

over 4000
2000-4000
1000-2000
400-1000
200-400
0-200

sea level

below sea
level

Key to map symbols

■ Over 5,000,000 inhabitants

● 1,000,000 - 5,000,000 inhabitants

• Under 1,000,000 inhabitants

Sofia   Capital cities underlined

Country boundaries

⸭ Historical sites   ⸭ Seasonal lakes

Scale 1:10 000 000   1 cm on the map = 100 km on the ground

0   250km   500km   750km   1000km

1   2   3   4   5   6   7   8   9   10
cm   cm   cm

BELARUS

POLAND
- dgoszcz
- Poznań
- Łódź
- Wrocław
- Katowice
- eten Highlands
- Brno

Vistula

Warsaw · Brest
Lublin
Kraków
Lvov

PUBLIC
SLOVAK REPUBLIC · Košice
enna
· Bratislava
Debrecen
HUNGARY
Lake Balaton
Budapest
az

Drava

Zagreb
ROATIA
Sava
Belgrade
BOSNIA-HERZEGOVINA
inaric Alps
· Sarajevo
lit
Dubrovnik
· Podgorica
Sea
· Bari
àranto

SERBIA
MONTE-NEGRO
· Priština
KOSOVO
· Skopje
MACEDONIA
· Tirane
ALBANIA

Pripet

Gomel
Chernigov
Chernobyl
Kiev · Dnieper
Zhitomir

Sumy
Kursk
Voronezh

Kharkov

U K R A I N E
Vinnitsa

Lvov
Chernovtsy

MOLDOVA
Iași
· Kishinev
Bacău
ROMANIA
Cluj-Napoca
Timișoara
Brașov
Transylvanian Alps
Ploiești
Bucharest

Danube

Varna
Balkan Mountains
Sofia
BULGARIA
Plovdiv
Rhodope Mountains

Burgas

Dnieper
Lugansk
Donetsk
Rostov

Don

Dnepropetrovsk
Krivoy Rog
Zaporozhye
Nikolayev
Mariupol

R U S S I A

Stavropol
Krasnodar

Bug

Odessa

Sea of Azov

Crimea
Sevastopol
Yalta

B l a c k   S e a

Caucasus
Sochi
Sukhumi
GEORGIA
Batumi

Constanța

Samsun
P o n t i n e   M o u n t a i n s
Trabzon
Zonguldak

Thasos

Istanbul · Izmit
Bosporus
Dardanelles · Troy
Lesbos

Bursa
Balıkeşir

Ankara
Eskişehir

Sivas

T U R K E Y

Kayseri

A S I A

Euphrates

Mount Olympus 2917
Pindus Mountains
Corfu (Greece)

Æg e a n
Sea
Sporades

GREECE
· Delphi
Marathon
Athens
· Olympia
Peloponnese
· Sparta

Gulf of Corinth
Patra

Hios
Samos
Cyclades

Dodecanese

Santorini

Manisa
Izmir
Denizli

Kos

Rhodes (Greece)

Isparta

Konya

Antalya

T a u r u s   M o u n t a i n s
Mersin

Adana
Gaziantep

Aleppo

SYRIA
Latakia
CYPRUS
· Nicosia
Limassol

Homs
Tripoli

LEBANON
Beirut
Damascus

Ionian Sea
Ionian Islands
essina
t of Messina

Iraklio
Knossos

Crete (Greece)

A e g e a n   S e a

Haifa
ISRAEL
Tel Aviv-Jaffa
Jerusalem
GAZA STRIP

WEST BANK
Amman

Dead Sea -022

JORDAN

E A N   S E A

· Benghazi
LIBYA

Gulf of Sidra

Alexandria

EGYPT

Port Said
Suez Canal
Ismâ'ilîya
Cairo

Sinai

COPYRIGHT PHILIP'S

Cross-section along latitude 45°N

FRANCE   ITALY   ROMANIA

Bay of Biscay
Mont Dore 1886
Massif Central
Rhone
Mont Blanc 4808 Alps
Po
Adriatic Sea
Dinaric Alps
Sava
Danube
Transylvanian Alps
Danube
Black Sea

45°N   45°N

cator map

Italy map

SWITZERLAND
LIECHTENSTEIN
AUSTRIA
SLOVENIA
CROATIA
FRANCE
MONACO

Mont Blanc 4808
Monte Rosa 4634
Dolomites
Bolzano
3342
Trento
Údine
Trieste

Lake Como
Lake Maggiore
Milan
Brescia
Bergamo
Novara
Lake Garda
Verona
Vicenza
Padua
Venice
Turin
Piacenza
Parma
Réggio
Ferrara
Po
Alessandria
Módena
Bologna
Genoa
Forli
Ravenna
Gulf of Genoa
La Spézia
SAN MARINO
Rímini
San Remo
Pisa
Florence
Riviera
Livorno
Siena
Ancona
Perúgia
Grosseto
Elba
Terni
2912
Pescara
Tiber
Celano
VATICAN CITY
Rome
Fóggia
Latina
Bari
Mount Vesuvius 1281
Naples
Pompeii
Bríndisi
Ischia
Salerno
Potenza
Táranto
Lecce
Capri
Sorrento
Gulf of Táranto
Cosenza
1928
Strómboli 924
Aeolian Islands
Messina
Réggio di Calabria
Palermo
Mount Etna 3323
Marsala
Sicily
Catánia
Siracusa
Pantelleria
Égadi Islands

Corsica (France)
Strait of Bonifacio
Sardinia (Italy)
Ólbia
Sássari
1834
Cágliari

Ligurian Sea
Adriatic Sea
Tyrrhenian Sea
Ionian Sea
Strait of Otranto

East from Greenwich

Strómboli

▲ **Strómboli**   Known as the 'Lighthouse of the Mediterranean', it is one of three active volcanoes in Italy. The others are Mount Etna and Mount Vesuvius.

Scale 1:6 250 000   1 cm on the map = 62.5 km on the ground

| 0 | 62.5km | 125km | 187.5km | 250km | 312.5km | 375km |

cm 1 2 3 4 5 6

Key to map symbols

- ■ Over 1,000,000 inhabitants
- ● 500,000 – 1,000,000 inhabitants
- ● Under 500,000 inhabitants
- **Rome** Capital cities
- ── Country boundaries
- ∴ Historical site

Height of the land (metres)

- over 4000
- 2000-4000
- 1000-2000
- 400-1000
- 200-400
- 0-200 (sea level)
- below sea level

Locator map

Venice

▼ **Venice** This image shows the largest island, on which the main part of the city is built. There are no roads so everything is moved by boat and you can see the wakes made by some of the larger boats.

REGION

VALLE D'AOSTA
ALTO ADIGE TRENTINO
PIEDMONT
LOMBARDY
VENETO
FRIULI-VENEZIA GIULIA
LIGURIA
EMILIA-ROMAGNA
TUSCANY
MARCHE
UMBRIA
ABRUZZO
LAZIO
MOLISE
SARDINIA
CAMPANIA
PUGLIA
BASILICATA
CALABRIA
SICILY

At the centre of this satellite image lies Italy, with the island of Sicily at its base. The snow-covered Alps can clearly be seen, forming the northern boundary of the country. To the west, in the Tyrrhenian Sea, are the islands of Corsica (to the north) and Sardinia.

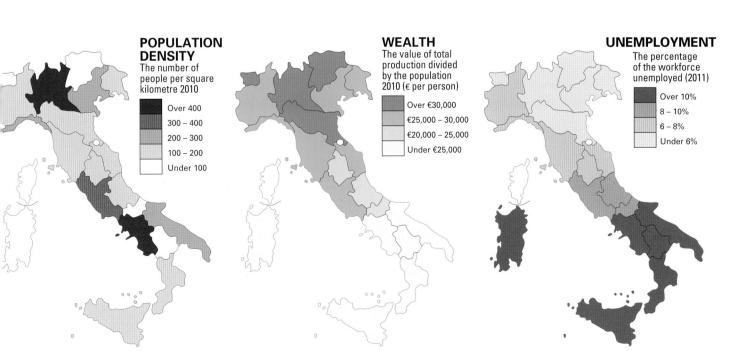

POPULATION DENSITY
The number of people per square kilometre 2010

- Over 400
- 300 – 400
- 200 – 300
- 100 – 200
- Under 100

WEALTH
The value of total production divided by the population 2010 (€ per person)

- Over €30,000
- €25,000 – 30,000
- €20,000 – 25,000
- Under €25,000

UNEMPLOYMENT
The percentage of the workforce unemployed (2011)

- Over 10%
- 8 – 10%
- 6 – 8%
- Under 6%

COPYRIGHT PHILIP'S

Height of the land (metres)

over 6000
4000–6000
2000–4000
1000–2000
400–1000
200–400
0–200
below sea level

sea level

Locator map

North America
Arctic Ocean
Pacific Ocean
Oceania
Europe
Africa
Indian Ocean

Scale 1:48 000 000

COPYRIGHT PHILIP'S

East from Greenwich

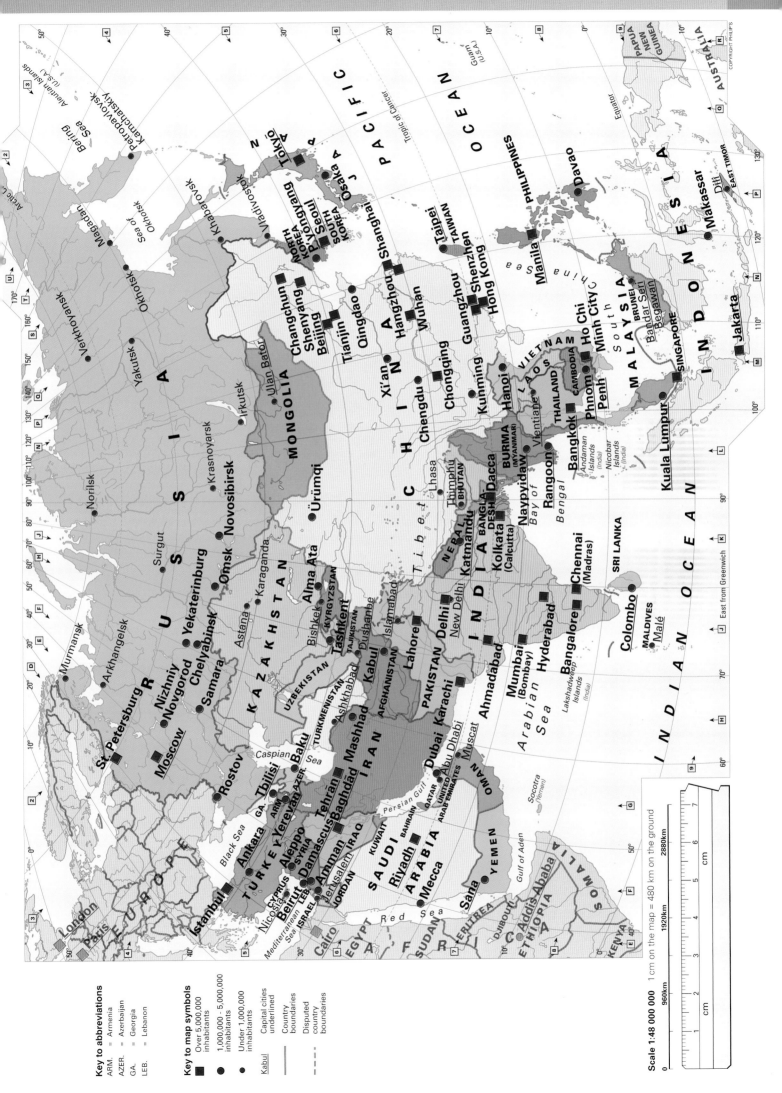

COPYRIGHT PHILIPS

Key to abbreviations

ARM. = Armenia
AZER. = Azerbaijan
GA. = Georgia
LEB. = Lebanon

Key to map symbols

■ Over 5,000,000 inhabitants

● 1,000,000 - 5,000,000 inhabitants

• Under 1,000,000 inhabitants

Kabul Capital cities underlined

——— Country boundaries

– – – Disputed country boundaries

Scale 1:48 000 000   1 cm on the map = 480 km on the ground

0   960km   1920km   2880km

Height of the land
(metres)

	over 6000
	4000-6000
	2000-4000
	1000-2000
	400-1000
	200-400
	0-200
sea level	
	below sea level

Key to map symbols

■ Over 5,000,000 inhabitants

● 1,000,000 - 5,000,000 inhabitants

• Under 1,000,000 inhabitants

<u>Kiev</u> Capital cities underlined

- - - Country boundaries

80° 90° 100° 110° 120° 130° 140° 150° 160° 80° 170° 180° 70° 60°

OCEAN

Komsomolets Island
October Revolution Island
Bolshevik Island

Severnaya
Zemlya

Boris Vilkitski Strait
Cape Chelyuskin

Laptev

Sea

New Siberian Islands

East Siberian Sea

Wrangel Island

Anadyr Range

Gulf of Anadyr

Lyakhov Islands
Dimiti Laptev Strait

Nizhne Kolymsk

Anadyr

Bering
Sea

Taimyr
Peninsula

Lake
Taimyr

• Nordvik

Olenek

Tiksi

Verkhoyansk Range

Kolyma Range

Kolyma

Gizhiga

• Khatanga

Yana

Indigirka

Cherskiy Range

Verkhoyansk

Oymyakon

Shelekhov
Gulf

Magadan

Sredinnyy Range

Kamchatka
Pen.

▲4750
Klyuchevskaya

• Norilsk

Central

Arctic Circle

Lena

Siberian

Vilyuy

Okhotsk

Sea of
Okhotsk

Petropavlovsk-
Kamchatskiy

Lower Tunguska

Plateau

Yakutsk

Aldan

Shantar Islands

Sakhalin

Aleksandrovsk-
Sakhalinskiy

Kuril Islands

50°

S *I* *A*

Olekminsk

Aldan

Yuzhno-
Sakhalinsk

Stony Tunguska

Angara

• Ust-Ilimsk

Vitim

Stanovoy Range

Zeya
Reservoir

Amur

Sikhote Alin Range

Asahikawa

Hokkaidō

Sapporo

5

b *e* *r* *i* *a*

Bratsk
Reservoir

Lena

Komsomolsk

Khabarovsk

Ussuri

• Kansk

Krasnoyarsk

• Bratsk

Yenisey

• Nizhneudinsk

Yablonovyy Range

Argun

Amur

Blagoveshchensk

Hegang

Sungari

Jiamusi

Lake Khanka

Vladivostok

Hakodate

40°

Sayan
Mountains

Abakan

Angara

Angarsk

Lake Baikal

Chita

Hailar

Daqing

Qiqihar

Jixi

Mudanjiang

Akita

Munku Sardyk
3491

Irkutsk

Ulan Ude

Manzhouli

CHINA

Fuyu

Harbin

Sapporo

Lake Uvs

Ulan Bator

Manchuria

Jilin

Sungari
Reservoir

Ch'ŏngjin

Sea of

Honshū

6

JAPAN

Sendai

Khangai Mountains

MONGOLIA

Changchun

Fushun

Kimch'aek

Japan

Tōkyō

Gobi

Chifeng

Shenyang

NORTH KOREA

P'yŏngyang

Yokohama

Nagoya

Desert

Inner
Mongolia

Anshan

Tangshan

Seoul

SOUTH KOREA

Kōbe

Ōsaka

n

K

100°

L

110°

M

120°

N

130°

P

COPYRIGHT PHILIP'S

Scale 1:20 000 000   1 cm on the map = 200 km on the ground

0   500km   1000km   1500km   2000km   2500km

cm   cm   cm

Locator map

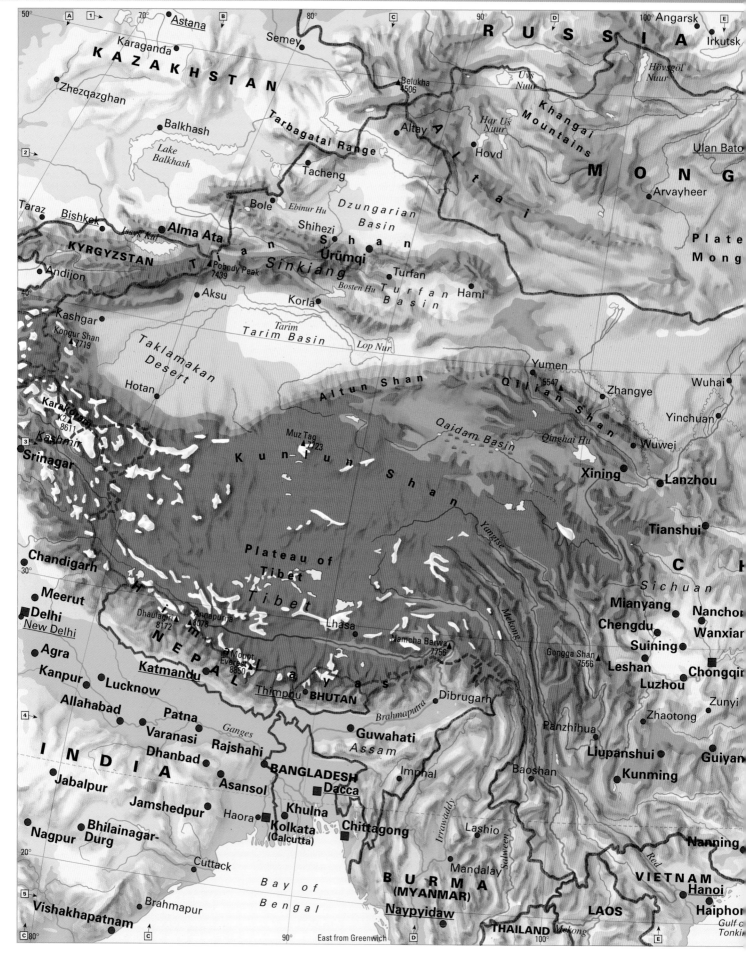

RUSSIA Angarsk
Irkutsk

K A Z A K H S T A N
Karaganda
Semey
Belukha 4506
Hövsgöl Nuur
Khangai Mountains
Zhezqazghan
Uvs Nuur
M O N G
Lake Balkhash
Balkhash
Tarbagatai Range
Altay
Altai
Har Us Nuur
Ulan Bato
Hovd
Arvayheer
P l a t e
M o n g
Taraz
Bishkek
Bole
Ebinur Hu
Dzungarian Basin
Alma Ata
Shihezi
T a n S h a n
Urümqi
KYRGYZSTAN
T S i n k i a n g
Andijon
Pobedy Peak 7439
Turfan Hami
Bosten Hu
Turfan Basin
Aksu
Korla
Kashgar
Tarim
Tarim Basin
Lop Nur
Yumen
Wuhai
Kongur Shan 7719
Taklamakan Desert
Qilian Shan
5547
Zhangye
Yinchuan
Karakoram
Hotan
Altun Shan
Qaidam Basin
Qinghai Hu
Wuwei
K2 8611
Muz Tag 7723
K u n l u n S h a n
Xining
Lanzhou
Kashmir
Srinagar
P l a t e a u of T i b e t
Yangtze
Tianshui
Chandigarh
T i b e t
Lhasa
C H
Meerut
Dhaulagiri 8172
Annapurna 8078
Namcha Barwa 7756
Mekong
S i c h u a n
Delhi
New Delhi
N E P A L
H i m a l a y a s
Gongga Shan 7556
Mianyang
Nanchor
Agra
Mount Everest 8850
Katmandu
Dibrugarh
Chengdu
Wanxiar
Kanpur
Lucknow
Thimphu
BHUTAN
Brahmaputra
Suining
Luzhou
Chongqir
Allahabad
Patna
Ganges
Guwahati
Assam
Panzhihua
Leshan
Zunyi
Varanasi
Rajshahi
Imphal
Zhaotong
I N D I A
Dhanbad
Asansol
BANGLADESH
Dacca
Baoshan
Liupanshui
Guiyan
Jabalpur
Khulna
Kunming
Jamshedpur
Haora
Kolkata (Calcutta)
Chittagong
Lashio
Nanning
Nagpur
Bhilainagar-Durg
Cuttack
Mandalay
Irrawaddy
Salween
VIETNAM
Brahmapur
B a y of B e n g a l
B U R M A (MYANMAR)
Hanoi
Vishakhapatnam
Naypyidaw
LAOS
Haiphon
THAILAND
Mekong
Gulf o Tonki

Scale 1:15 000 000 1 cm on the map = 150 km on the ground

0   300km   600km   900km   1200km   1500km

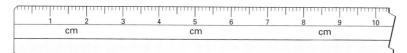

cm   cm   cm

Height of the land (metres)

	over 6000
	4000-6000
	2000-4000
	1000-2000
	400-1000
	200-400
sea level	0-200
	below sea level

Key to map symbols

■ Over 5,000,000 inhabitants

● 1,000,000 - 5,000,000 inhabitants

• Under 1,000,000 inhabitants

Beijing Capital cities underlined

━━━ Country boundaries

▃▃▃ Disputed country boundaries

Locator map

COPYRIGHT PHILIP'S

INDUSTRIAL REGIONS

- Core industrial regions
- Major centres for industry
- Centres for iron and steel, and chemicals
- Rapidly developing coastal regions
- Special Economic Zones
- Special Administrative Regions
- Outer industrial regions
- Outer industrial regions with traditional heavy industry
- Remote undeveloped regions
- Direction of future growth
- Important rail links

Ürümqi
Kashi
Baotou
Beijing
Tianjin
Dalian
Taiyuan
Qingdao
Lanzhou
Zhengzhou
Xi'an
Pudong
Three Gorges Dam
Nanjing
Shanghai
Chongqing
Wuhan
Ningbo
Changsha
Wenzhou
Chengdu
Fuzhou
Xiamen
Guangzhou (Canton)
Shantou
Zhuhai
Shenzhen
Macau
Hong Kong
Hainan
Harbin
Changchun
Fushun
Shenyang

EMPLOYMENT IN INDUSTRY

Industrial workforce by province in millions

6 4 2 1 0.5

Income by province – the value of total production divided by the population in US$ 2010

- Over $10,000
- $5,000 – $10,000
- $2,500 – $5,000
- Under $2,500

SINKIANG
HEILONGJIANG
JILIN
INNER MONGOLIA
LIAONING
GANSU
BEIJING
QINGHAI
NINGXIA HUI
HEBEI
TIANJIN
SHANDONG
SHANXI
SHAANXI
SICHUAN
HENAN
JIANGSU
TIBET
CHONGQING
HUBEI
ANHUI
SHANGHAI
ZHEJIANG
HUNAN
JIANGXI
YUNNAN
GUIZHOU
FUJIAN
GUANGXI ZHUANGZU
GUANGDONG
MACAU
HONG KONG
HAINAN

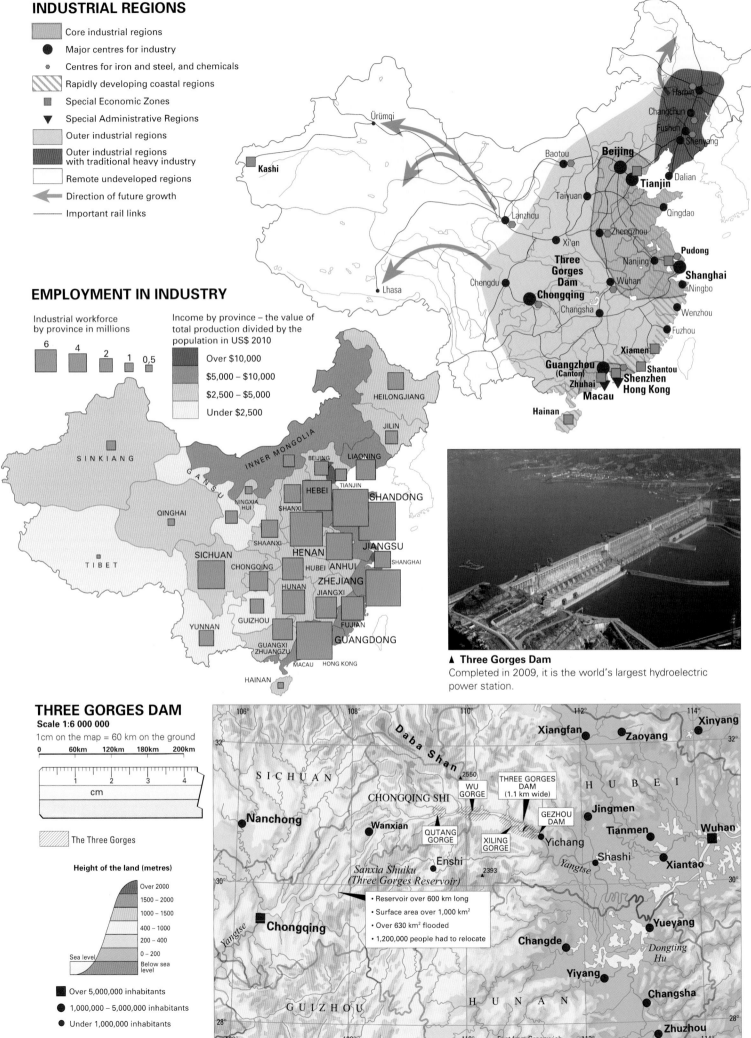

▲ Three Gorges Dam
Completed in 2009, it is the world's largest hydroelectric power station.

THREE GORGES DAM

Scale 1:6 000 000
1cm on the map = 60 km on the ground

0   60km   120km   180km   200km

cm

The Three Gorges

Height of the land (metres)

- Over 2000
- 1500 – 2000
- 1000 – 1500
- 400 – 1000
- 200 – 400
- 0 – 200
- Sea level / Below sea level

- Over 5,000,000 inhabitants
- 1,000,000 – 5,000,000 inhabitants
- Under 1,000,000 inhabitants

Daba Shan
Xiangfan
Zaoyang
Xinyang
SICHUAN
CHONGQING SHI
WU GORGE
2550
THREE GORGES DAM (1.1 km wide)
HUBEI
Jingmen
Nanchong
Wanxian
QUTANG GORGE
GEZHOU DAM
Tianmen
Wuhan
XILING GORGE
Yichang
Shashi
Xiantao
Enshi
2393
Yangtse
Sanxia Shuiku (Three Gorges Reservoir)
Chongqing
Yangtse
Yueyang
Dongting Hu
Changde
Yiyang
Changsha
GUIZHOU
HUNAN
Zhuzhou

- Reservoir over 600 km long
- Surface area over 1,000 km²
- Over 630 km² flooded
- 1,200,000 people had to relocate

COPYRIGHT PHILIP'S

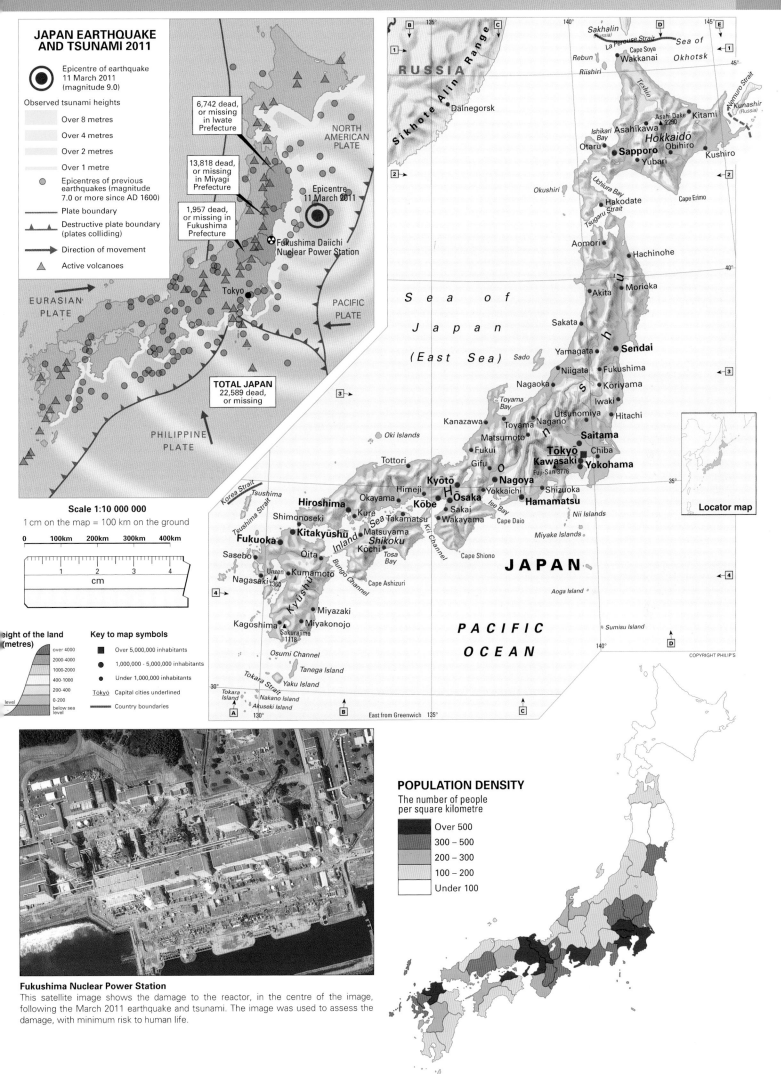

JAPAN EARTHQUAKE AND TSUNAMI 2011

Epicentre of earthquake
11 March 2011
(magnitude 9.0)

Observed tsunami heights

Over 8 metres

Over 4 metres

Over 2 metres

Over 1 metre

Epicentres of previous earthquakes (magnitude 7.0 or more since AD 1600)

Plate boundary

Destructive plate boundary (plates colliding)

Direction of movement

Active volcanoes

6,742 dead, or missing in Iwate Prefecture

13,818 dead, or missing in Miyagi Prefecture

1,957 dead, or missing in Fukushima Prefecture

Epicentre 11 March 2011

Fukushima Daiichi Nuclear Power Station

Tokyo

NORTH AMERICAN PLATE

PACIFIC PLATE

EURASIAN PLATE

PHILIPPINE PLATE

TOTAL JAPAN
22,589 dead, or missing

Scale 1:10 000 000
1 cm on the map = 100 km on the ground

| 0 | 100km | 200km | 300km | 400km |

| 1 | 2 | 3 | 4 |
cm

Height of the land (metres)

over 4000
2000-4000
1000-2000
400-1000
200-400
0-200
below sea level

sea level

Key to map symbols

Over 5,000,000 inhabitants

1,000,000 - 5,000,000 inhabitants

Under 1,000,000 inhabitants

Tokyo Capital cities underlined

Country boundaries

RUSSIA

Sikhote Alin Range

Dalnegorsk

Sakhalin (Russia)

La Perouse Strait

Cape Soya
Wakkanai

Sea of Okhotsk

Rebun
Riishiri

Teshio

Kunashir (Russia)

Nemuro Strait

Asahi Dake 2290
Kitami

Ishikari Bay
Asahikawa
Otaru

Hokkaidō

Sapporo
Obihiro
Yubari
Kushiro

Okushiri

Uchiura Bay

Hakodate
Tsugaru Strait

Cape Erimo

Aomori

Hachinohe

Akita
Morioka

Sea of Japan (East Sea)

Sakata

Sado

Yamagata
Sendai

Niigata
Fukushima

Nagaoka
Kōriyama

Toyama Bay
Iwaki

Kanazawa
Toyama
Nagano
Utsunomiya
Hitachi

Matsumoto

Fukui
Saitama

Gifu
Tōkyō
Chiba

Nagoya
Kawasaki
Yokohama

Tottori
Yokkaichi
Shizuoka

Himeji
Okayama
Kōbe
Ōsaka
Fuji-San 3776
Hamamatsu

Hiroshima
Kure
Sakai
Cape Daio

Shimonoseki
Takamatsu
Wakayama

Sea
Matsuyama

Kitakyūshū
Shikoku
Kōchi

Fukuoka
Ōita
Inland
Tosa Bay

Sasebo
Bungo Channel
Cape Shiono

Unzen 1360
Kumamoto
Cape Ashizuri

Nagasaki

Miyazaki
Miyakonojo

Kagoshima
Sakurajima 1118

Osumi Channel

Tanega Island

Tokara Strait
Yaku Island

Tokara Island
Nakano Island
Akuseki Island

Korea Strait
Tsushima
Tsushima Strait

Tsushima Strait

Oki Islands

Nii Islands

Miyake Islands

JAPAN

Aoga Island

Sumisu Island

PACIFIC OCEAN

East from Greenwich 135°

Kyūshū

Locator map

COPYRIGHT PHILIP'S

Fukushima Nuclear Power Station
This satellite image shows the damage to the reactor, in the centre of the image, following the March 2011 earthquake and tsunami. The image was used to assess the damage, with minimum risk to human life.

POPULATION DENSITY
The number of people per square kilometre

Over 500

300 – 500

200 – 300

100 – 200

Under 100

Cross-section along latitude 30°N

IRAN   PAKISTAN   INDIA   TIBET   CHINA

Height of the land (metres)

	over 6000
	4000-6000
	2000-4000
	1000-2000
	400-1000
	200-400
	0-200
sea level	
	below sea level

Locator map

COPYRIGHT PHILIP'S

Key to map symbols

■ Over 5,000,000 inhabitants

● 1,000,000 - 5,000,000 inhabitants

• Under 1,000,000 inhabitants

Beijing Capital cities underlined

━━━━ Country boundaries

- - - - Disputed country boundaries

Seasonal lakes

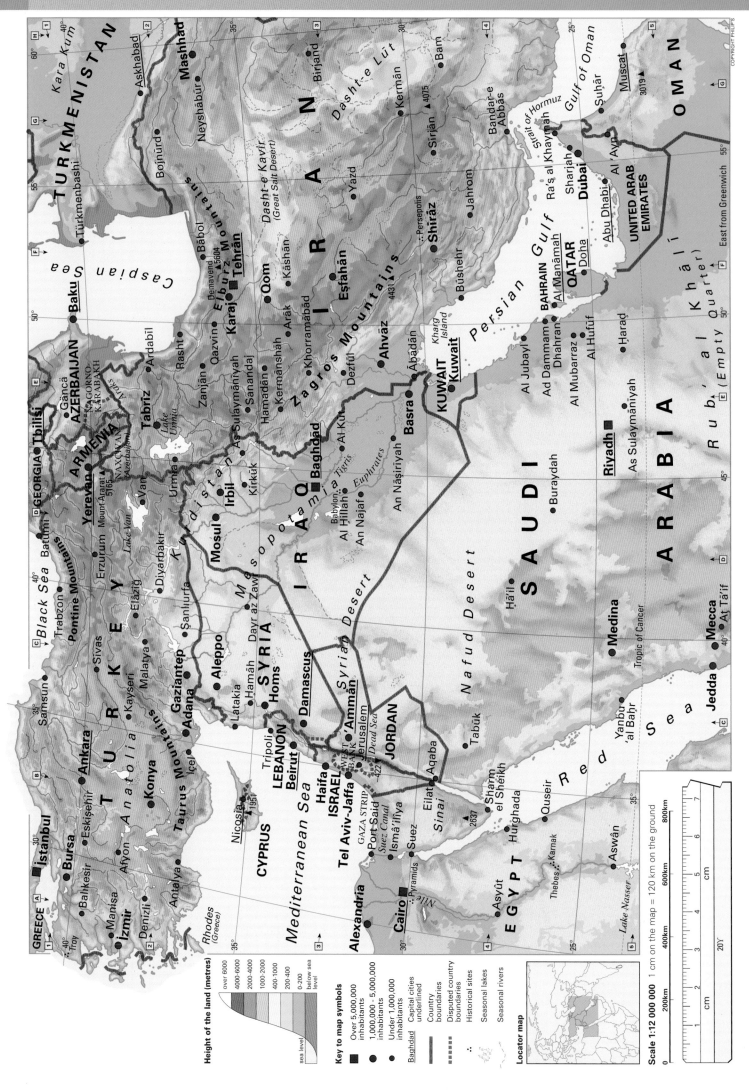

Height of the land (metres)

over 6000
4000-6000
2000-4000
1000-2000
400-1000
200-400
0-200
below sea level

sea level

Key to map symbols

Over 5,000,000 inhabitants

1,000,000 - 5,000,000 inhabitants

Under 1,000,000 inhabitants

Baghdad   Capital cities underlined

Country boundaries

Disputed country boundaries

Historical sites

Seasonal lakes

Seasonal rivers

Scale 1:12 000 000   1 cm on the map = 120 km on the ground

Locator map

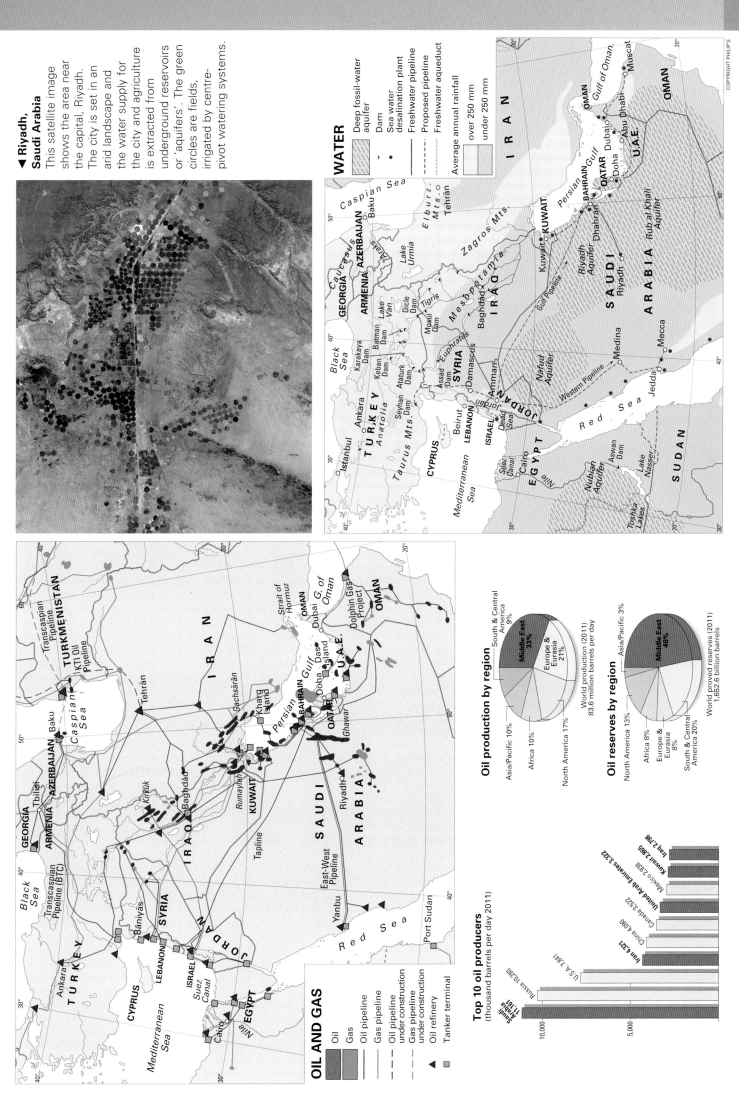

▲ **Riyadh, Saudi Arabia**
This satellite image shows the area near the capital, Riyadh. The city is set in an arid landscape and the water supply for the city and agriculture is extracted from underground reservoirs or 'aquifers'. The green circles are fields, irrigated by centre-pivot watering systems.

WATER

Deep fossil-water aquifer
Dam
Sea water desalination plant
Freshwater pipeline
Proposed pipeline
Freshwater aqueduct
Average annual rainfall
over 250 mm
under 250 mm

OIL AND GAS

Oil
Gas
Oil pipeline
Gas pipeline
Oil pipeline under construction
Gas pipeline under construction
Oil refinery
Tanker terminal

Oil production by region

South & Central America 9%
Middle East 33%
Europe & Eurasia 21%
Asia/Pacific 10%
Africa 10%
North America 17%

World production (2011) 83.6 million barrels per day

Oil reserves by region

Asia/Pacific 3%
Middle East 48%
North America 13%
Africa 8%
Europe & Eurasia 8%
South & Central America 20%

World proved reserves (2011) 1,652.6 billion barrels

Top 10 oil producers (thousand barrels per day 2011)

Saudi Arabia 11,161
Russia 10,280
U.S.A. 7,841
Iran 4,321
China 4,090
Canada 3,522
United Arab Emirates 3,322
Mexico 2,938
Kuwait 2,865
Iraq 2,798

COPYRIGHT PHILIP'S

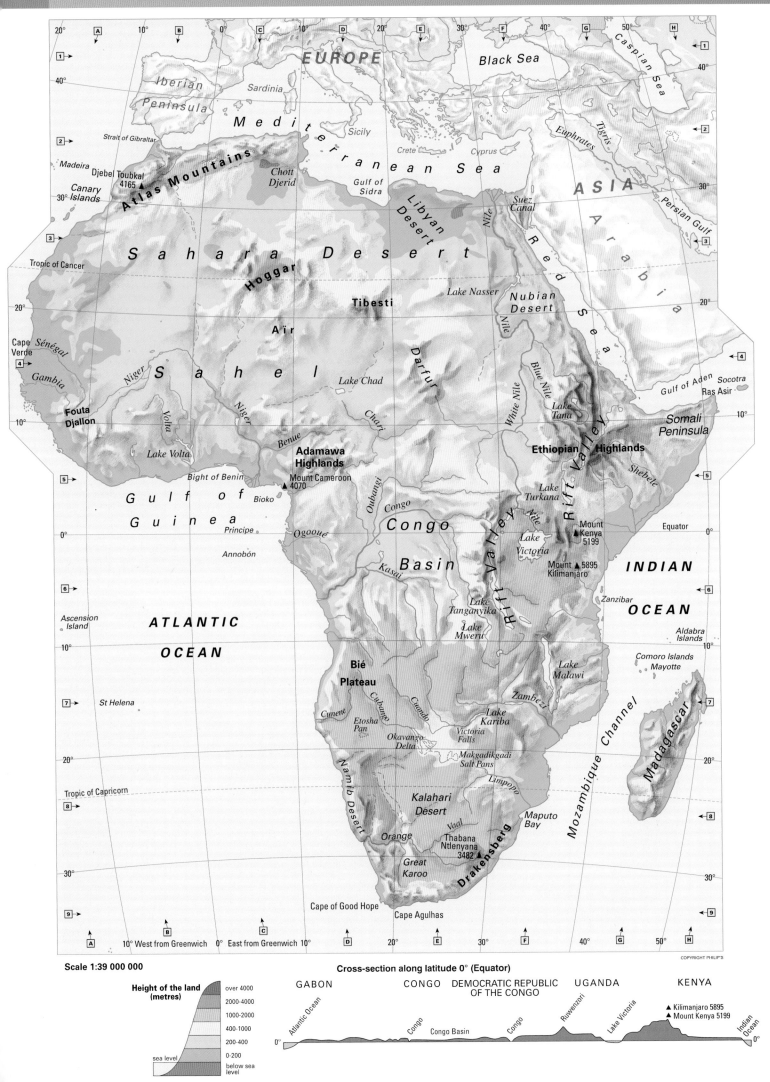

EUROPE

Black Sea

Caspian Sea

Iberian Peninsula

Sardinia

Sicily

M e d i t e r r a n e a n   S e a

Crete

Cyprus

Euphrates

Tigris

Madeira

Djebel Toubkal
4165

Strait of Gibraltar

Atlas Mountains

Chott Djerid

Gulf of Sidra

Libyan Desert

Suez Canal

A S I A

Red Sea

Persian Gulf

Canary Islands

30°

S a h a r a   D e s e r t

Tropic of Cancer

Hoggar

Tibesti

Lake Nasser

Nubian Desert

Aïr

Nile

A r a b i a

Nile

Cape Verde

Sénégal

Niger

S a h e l

Lake Chad

Darfur

White Nile

Blue Nile

Gulf of Aden

Socotra

Ras Asir

Gambia

Fouta Djallon

Volta

Niger

Chari

Benue

Lake Tana

Ethiopian Highlands

Somali Peninsula

Shebele

Lake Volta

Adamawa Highlands

Mount Cameroon
▲ 4070

Bight of Benin

Oubangi

Congo

Rift Valley

Atba

Lake Turkana

Mount Kenya
5199 ▲

G u l f   o f

Bioko

Principe

Ogooué

C o n g o

Mount Kilimanjaro
5895 ▲

Equator

G u i n e a

Annobón

Kasai

B a s i n

Rift Valley

Lake Victoria

I N D I A N

Zanzibar

A T L A N T I C

Ascension Island

Lake Tanganyika

Lake Mweru

O C E A N

Aldabra Islands

O C E A N

Comoro Islands

Mayotte

Bié Plateau

Lake Malawi

St Helena

Cunene

Cubango

Cuando

Zambezi

Lake Kariba

Victoria Falls

Etosha Pan

Okavango Delta

Makgadikgadi Salt Pans

Limpopo

Mozambique Channel

Madagascar

Tropic of Capricorn

Namib Desert

Kalahari Desert

Vaal

Thabana Ntlenyana
3482

Maputo Bay

Orange

Drakensberg

Great Karoo

Cape of Good Hope

Cape Agulhas

COPYRIGHT PHILIP'S

Scale 1:39 000 000

Height of the land (metres)

over 4000
2000–4000
1000–2000
400–1000
200–400
0–200

sea level

below sea level

Cross-section along latitude 0° (Equator)

GABON

CONGO

DEMOCRATIC REPUBLIC OF THE CONGO

UGANDA

KENYA

Atlantic Ocean

Congo

Congo Basin

Congo

Ruwenzori

Lake Victoria

▲ Kilimanjaro 5895
▲ Mount Kenya 5199

Indian Ocean

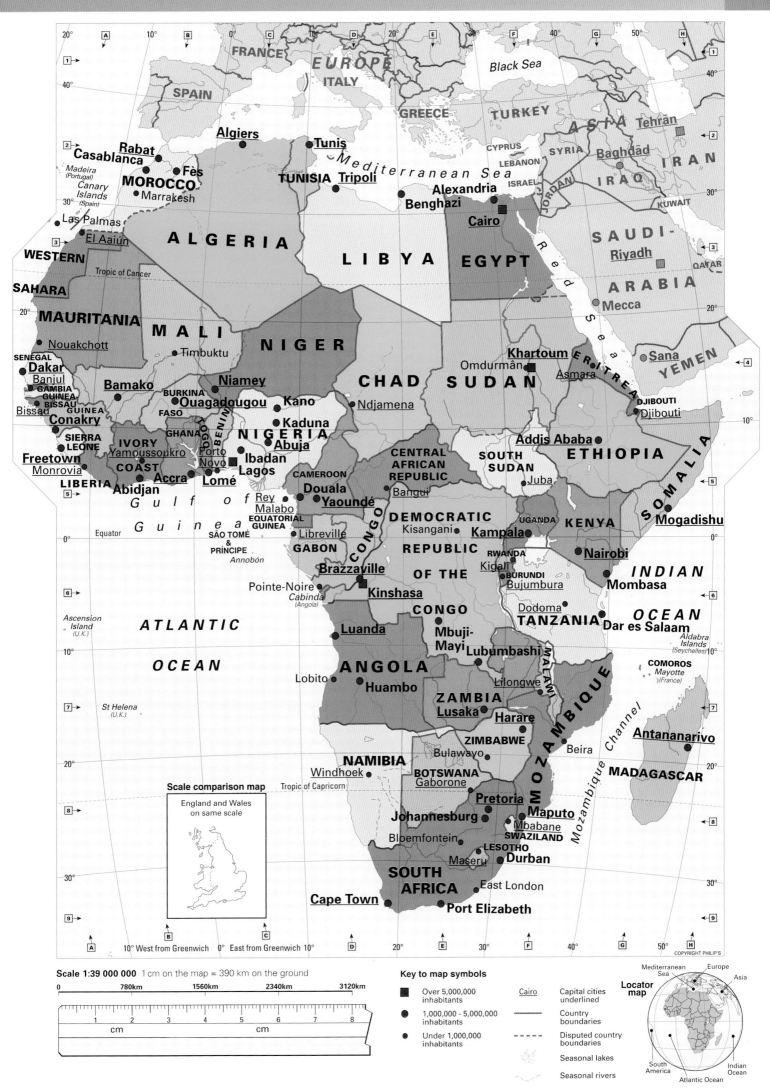

Scale 1:39 000 000 1 cm on the map = 390 km on the ground

0	780km	1560km	2340km	3120km

Key to map symbols

■ Over 5,000,000 inhabitants

● 1,000,000 – 5,000,000 inhabitants

• Under 1,000,000 inhabitants

Cairo Capital cities underlined

———— Country boundaries

- - - - Disputed country boundaries

Seasonal lakes

Seasonal rivers

Locator map

COPYRIGHT PHILIP'S

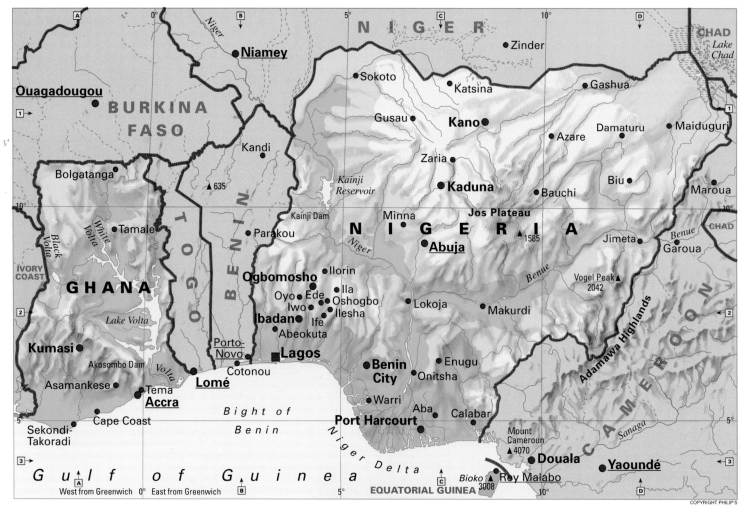

NIGERIA AND GHANA

Scale 1:10 000 000 1 cm on the map = 100 km on the ground

| 0 | 100km | 200km | 300km | 400km | 500km | 600km |

See page opposite for key to map symbols, locator map and height of the land reference panel.

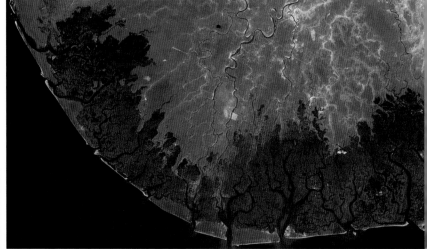

Niger Delta, Nigeria ▲

Satellite imagery helps to plan the drilling for oil and gas in the delta and to monitor the effect of the drilling on this fragile environment. This is a false colour image which shows vegetation such as mangrove swamps in dark red.

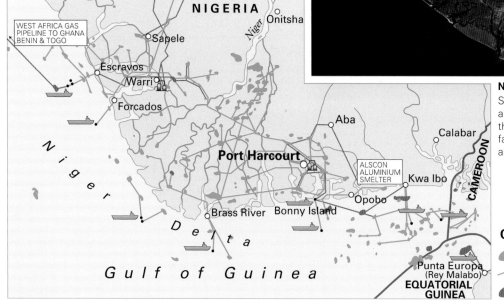

OIL AND GAS IN THE NIGER DELTA

Symbol		Symbol	
	Oilfields		Gas pipelines
	Oil pipelines		Tanker terminals
	Gasfields		Oil refineries

COPYRIGHT PHILIP'S

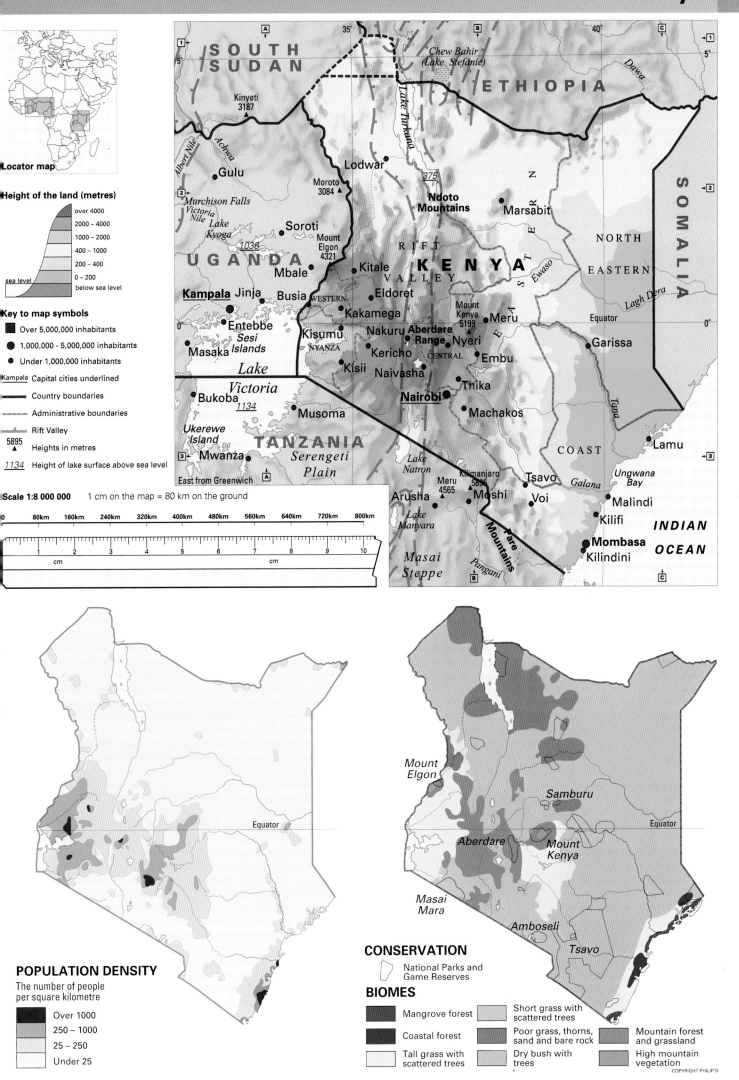

Locator map

Height of the land (metres)

- over 4000
- 2000 – 4000
- 1000 – 2000
- 400 – 1000
- 200 – 400
- 0 – 200
- sea level
- below sea level

Key to map symbols

- Over 5,000,000 inhabitants
- 1,000,000 - 5,000,000 inhabitants
- Under 1,000,000 inhabitants
- *Kampala* Capital cities underlined
- Country boundaries
- Administrative boundaries
- Rift Valley
- 5895 ▲ Heights in metres
- *1134* Height of lake surface above sea level

Scale 1:8 000 000   1 cm on the map = 80 km on the ground

0   80km   160km   240km   320km   400km   480km   560km   640km   720km   800km

SOUTH SUDAN

ETHIOPIA

Chew Bahir
(Lake Stefanie)

Kinyeti 3187

Gulu

Lodwar

Moroto 3084 ▲

Ndoto Mountains

Marsabit

Murchison Falls
Victoria Nile

Lake Kyoga

Soroti

Mount Elgon 4321

RIFT

KENYA

VALLEY

SOMALIA

NORTH EASTERN

UGANDA

Mbale

Kitale

Eldoret

Lagh Dera

Kampala   Jinja   Busia   WESTERN

Entebbe

Sesi Islands

Kakamega

Kisumu

NYANZA

Nakuru   Aberdare Range   Nyeri

Mount Kenya 5199   Meru

Equator

Masaka

Kericho

CENTRAL

Embu

Garissa

Lake Victoria 1134

Kisii

Naivasha

Bukoba

Thika

Nairobi

Machakos

COAST

Lamu

Musoma

Ungwana Bay

Ukerewe Island

TANZANIA

Serengeti Plain

Lake Natron

Lake Manyara

Meru 4565 ▲

Kilimanjaro 5895

Moshi

Arusha

Tsavo

Voi

Galana

Malindi

Kilifi

Tare Mountains

Mombasa
Kilindini

INDIAN OCEAN

Masai Steppe

Pangani

East from Greenwich

Albert Nile
Achwa
Lake Turkana
Dawa
Ewaso
Tana

POPULATION DENSITY

The number of people per square kilometre

- Over 1000
- 250 – 1000
- 25 – 250
- Under 25

Equator

CONSERVATION

National Parks and Game Reserves

Mount Elgon

Samburu

Aberdare

Mount Kenya

Masai Mara

Amboseli

Tsavo

BIOMES

- Mangrove forest
- Coastal forest
- Tall grass with scattered trees
- Short grass with scattered trees
- Poor grass, thorns, sand and bare rock
- Dry bush with trees
- Mountain forest and grassland
- High mountain vegetation

COPYRIGHT PHILIP'S

Cross-section along longitude 147°E — AUSTRALIA

North — Great Barrier Reef — Great Divide — Darling — Murray — Mount Kosciuszko 2228 — Snowy Mountains — Bass Strait — Tasmania — South
147°E ... 147°E

Height of the land (metres)

- over 4000
- 2000-4000
- 1000-2000
- 400-1000
- 200-400
- 0-200
- sea level
- below sea level

Key to map symbols

- Over 5,000,000 inhabitants
- 1,000,000 - 5,000,000 inhabitants
- Under 1,000,000 inhabitants
- Canberra Capital cities underlined
- Country boundaries
- State boundaries
- Seasonal lakes
- Seasonal rivers

Locator map

Asia — Pacific Ocean
Indian Ocean — Southern Ocean
Antarctica

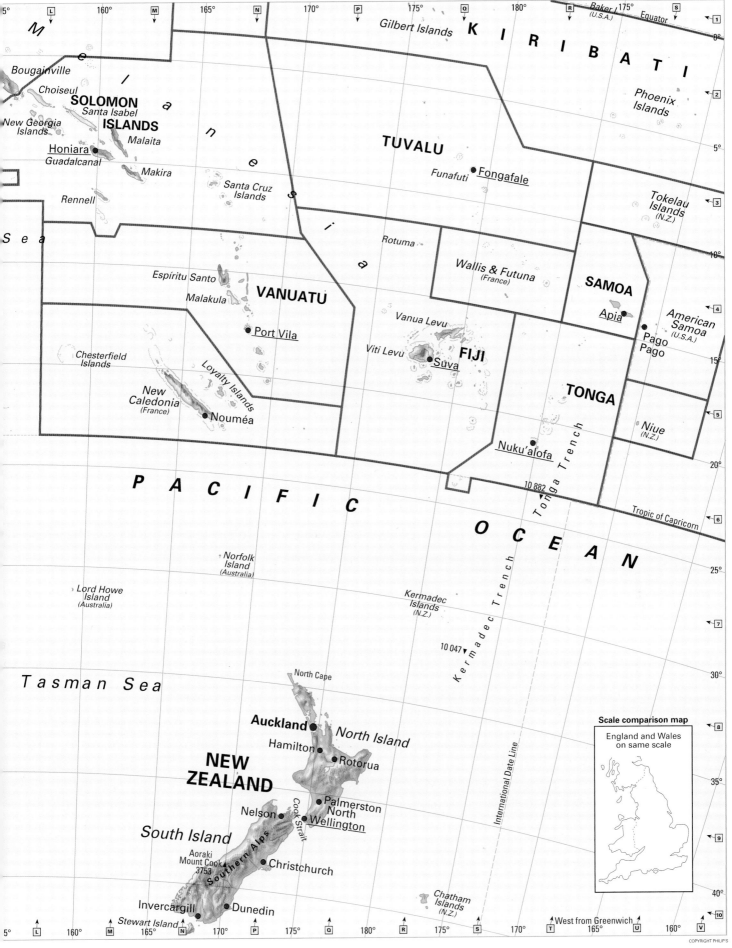

Scale 1:20 000 000   1 cm on the map = 200 km on the ground

0   500km   1000km   1500km   2000km

COPYRIGHT PHILIP'S

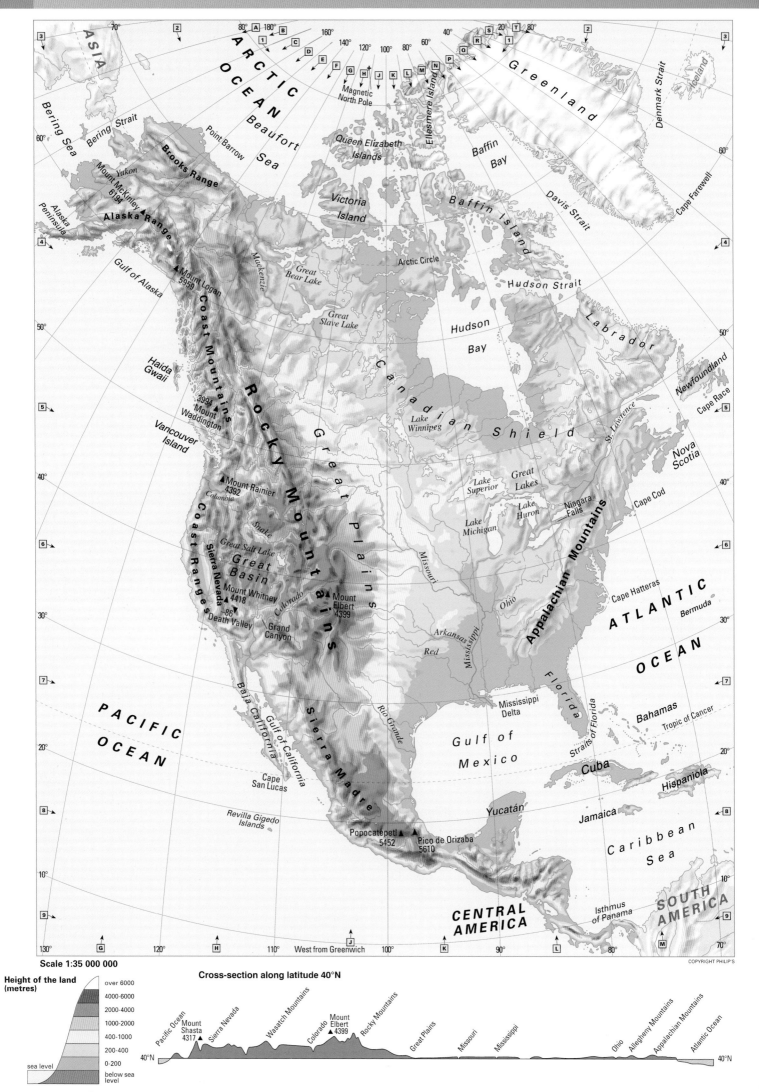

Scale 1:35 000 000

COPYRIGHT PHILIP'S

Height of the land (metres)

- over 6000
- 4000-6000
- 2000-4000
- 1000-2000
- 400-1000
- 200-400
- 0-200
- sea level
- below sea level

Cross-section along latitude 40°N

40°N — Pacific Ocean — Mount Shasta 4317 — Sierra Nevada — Wasatch Mountains — Colorado — Mount Elbert 4399 — Rocky Mountains — Great Plains — Missouri — Mississippi — Ohio — Allegheny Mountains — Appalachian Mountains — Atlantic Ocean — 40°N

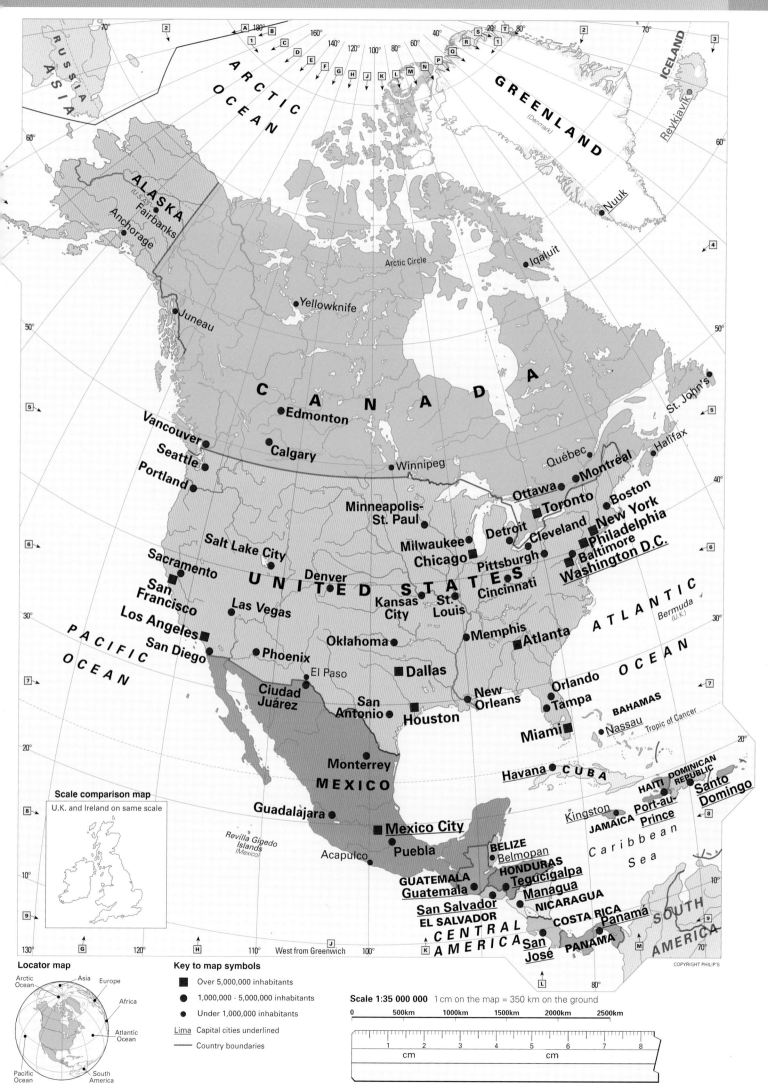

Scale comparison map

U.K. and Ireland on same scale

Locator map

Arctic Ocean
Asia
Europe
Africa
Atlantic Ocean
South America
Pacific Ocean
North America

Key to map symbols

■ Over 5,000,000 inhabitants

● 1,000,000 - 5,000,000 inhabitants

• Under 1,000,000 inhabitants

<u>Lima</u> Capital cities underlined

----- Country boundaries

Scale 1:35 000 000   1 cm on the map = 350 km on the ground

0   500km   1000km   1500km   2000km   2500km

COPYRIGHT PHILIP'S

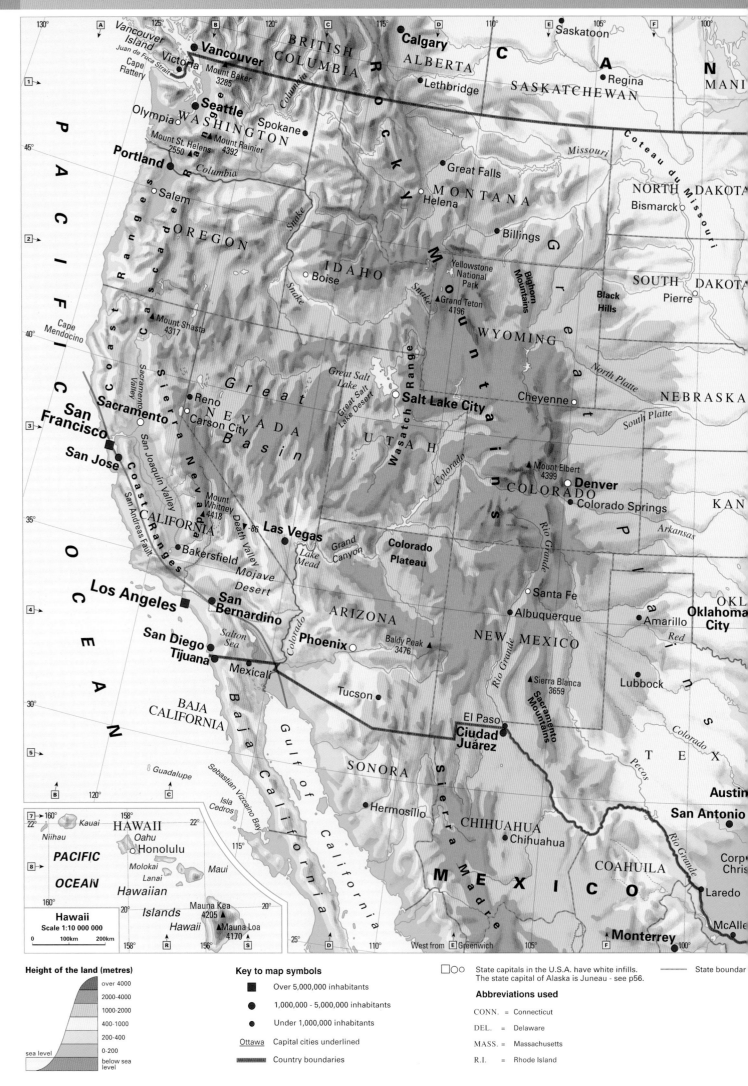

Height of the land (metres)

over 4000
2000-4000
1000-2000
400-1000
200-400
0-200
below sea level

sea level

Key to map symbols

■ Over 5,000,000 inhabitants

● 1,000,000 - 5,000,000 inhabitants

• Under 1,000,000 inhabitants

<u>Ottawa</u> Capital cities underlined

━━━ Country boundaries

☐○○ State capitals in the U.S.A. have white infills.
The state capital of Alaska is Juneau - see p56.

──── State boundar

Abbreviations used

CONN. = Connecticut

DEL. = Delaware

MASS. = Massachusetts

R.I. = Rhode Island

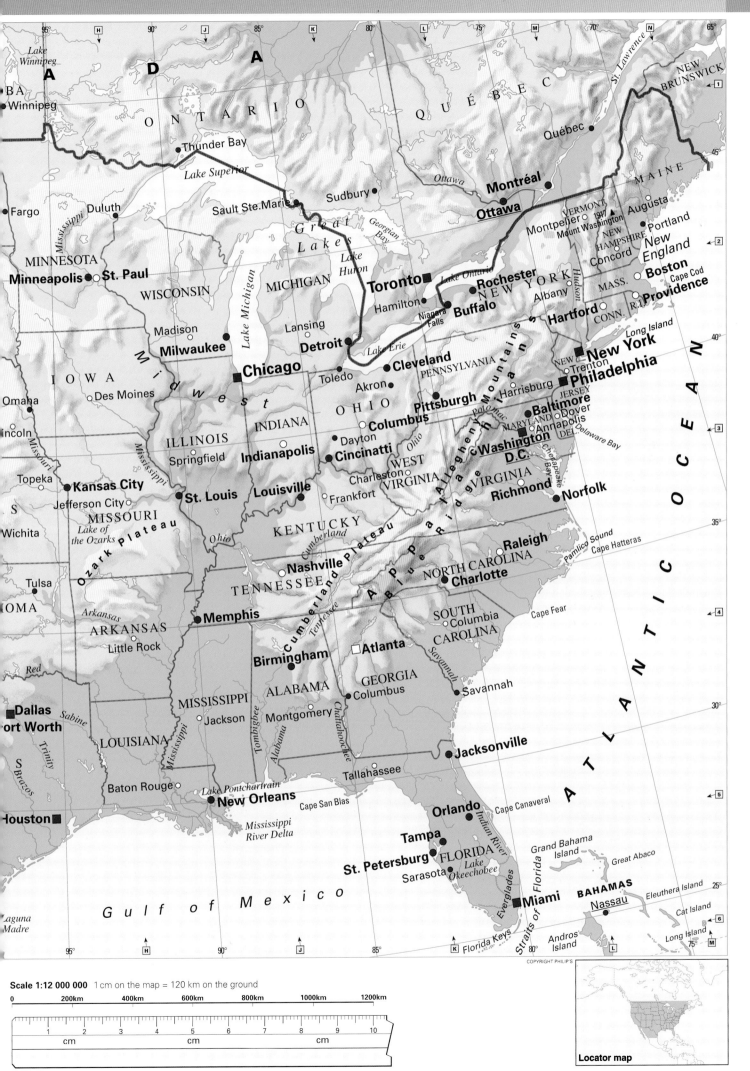

Scale 1:12 000 000   1 cm on the map = 120 km on the ground

| 0 | 200km | 400km | 600km | 800km | 1000km | 1200km |

COPYRIGHT PHILIP'S

Locator map

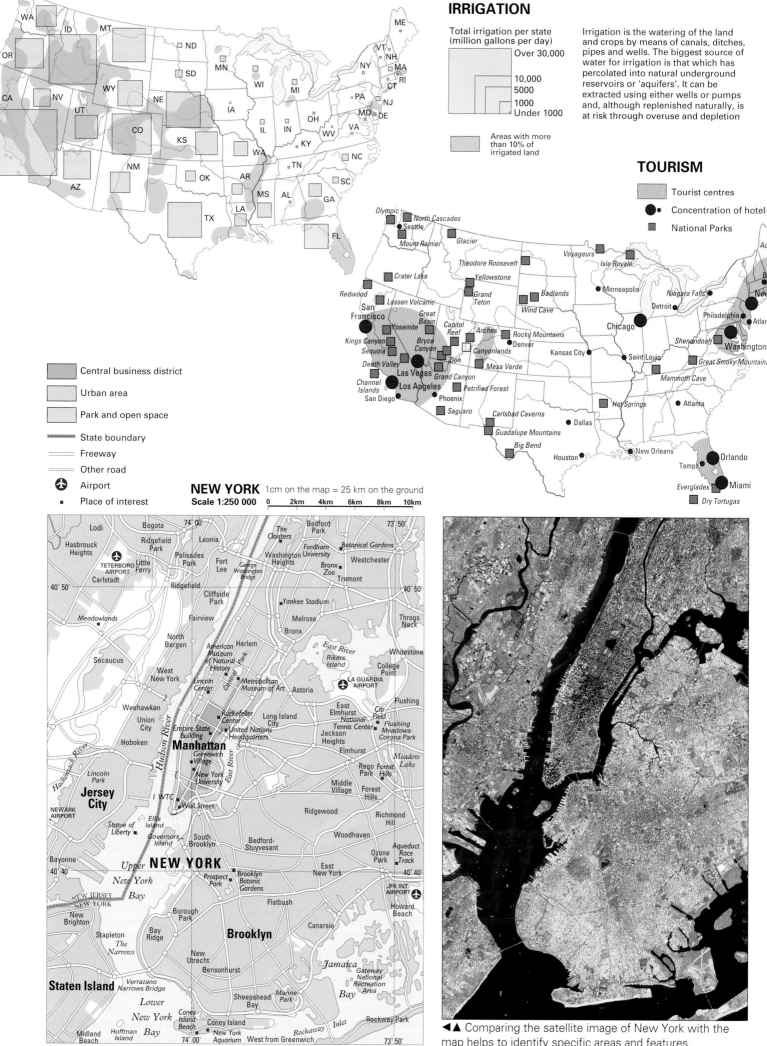

IRRIGATION

Total irrigation per state (million gallons per day)

Over 30,000
10,000
5000
1000
Under 1000

Irrigation is the watering of the land and crops by means of canals, ditches, pipes and wells. The biggest source of water for irrigation is that which has percolated into natural underground reservoirs or 'aquifers'. It can be extracted using either wells or pumps and, although replenished naturally, is at risk through overuse and depletion

Areas with more than 10% of irrigated land

TOURISM

Tourist centres
Concentration of hotel
National Parks

Central business district
Urban area
Park and open space
State boundary
Freeway
Other road
Airport
Place of interest

NEW YORK
Scale 1:250 000   1cm on the map = 25 km on the ground

0   2km   4km   6km   8km   10km

COPYRIGHT PHILIP'S

◄▲ Comparing the satellite image of New York with the map helps to identify specific areas and features.

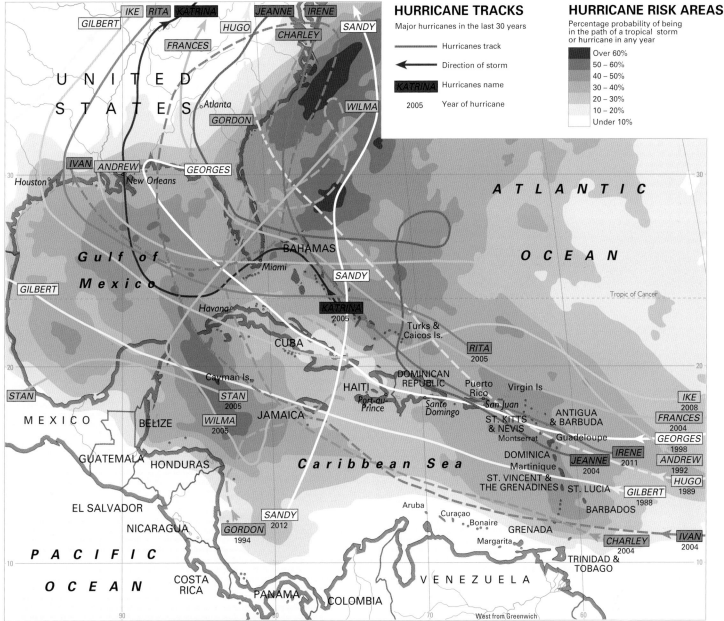

HURRICANE TRACKS

Major hurricanes in the last 30 years

- - - - - - Hurricanes track

⟵ Direction of storm

KATRINA Hurricanes name

2005 Year of hurricane

HURRICANE RISK AREAS

Percentage probability of being in the path of a tropical storm or hurricane in any year

- Over 60%
- 50 – 60%
- 40 – 50%
- 30 – 40%
- 20 – 30%
- 10 – 20%
- Under 10%

IKE RITA KATRINA JEANNE IRENE
GILBERT HUGO SANDY
FRANCES CHARLEY

U N I T E D

S T A T E S   *Atlanta*   *WILMA*

GORDON

IVAN ANDREW GEORGES

30   *Houston*   *New Orleans*   30

A T L A N T I C

Gulf of   BAHAMAS   O C E A N

Mexico   *Miami*

GILBERT   *SANDY*   Tropic of Cancer

Havana   *KATRINA*
2005

CUBA   Turks & Caicos Is.

20   *RITA*   20
2005

Cayman Is.   DOMINICAN REPUBLIC   Puerto   Virgin Is
                                    Rico
STAN   HAITI   *San Juan*   *IKE*
                Port-au-   Santo   2008
MEXICO   *STAN*   Prince   Domingo   ST. KITTS   ANTIGUA   *FRANCES*
        2005   & NEVIS   & BARBUDA   2004
BELIZE   *WILMA*   JAMAICA   Montserrat   Guadeloupe   *GEORGES*
        2005   1998
                                DOMINICA   *JEANNE IRENE*   *ANDREW*
GUATEMALA   HONDURAS   Caribbean Sea   Martinique   2004   2011   1992
                            ST. VINCENT &   *HUGO*
                            THE GRENADINES   ST. LUCIA   *GILBERT*   1989
EL SALVADOR   Aruba   1988
                                    Curaçao   BARBADOS
NICARAGUA   *SANDY*   2012   Bonaire   GRENADA
        GORDON   Margarita   *CHARLEY*   *IVAN*
10   1994   2004   2004   10
P A C I F I C   TRINIDAD &
                                    TOBAGO
O C E A N   COSTA   V E N E Z U E L A
            RICA   PANAMA   COLOMBIA
                        West from Greenwich

▲ Hurricane Katrina hit the USA's Gulf Coast on 29 August 2005. It was the costliest and one of the five deadliest hurricanes ever to strike the United States. This satellite image shows the storm approaching the US coastline.

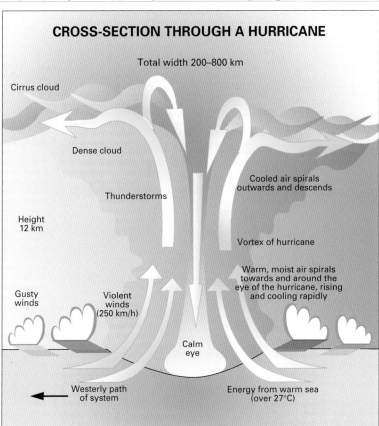

CROSS-SECTION THROUGH A HURRICANE

Total width 200–800 km

Cirrus cloud

Dense cloud

Cooled air spirals outwards and descends

Thunderstorms

Vortex of hurricane

Height
12 km

Warm, moist air spirals towards and around the eye of the hurricane, rising and cooling rapidly

Gusty   Violent
winds   winds
        (250 km/h)

Calm
eye

Westerly path   Energy from warm sea
of system   (over 27°C)

COPYRIGHT PHILIP'S

Scale comparison map

England and Wales on same scale

Height of the land (metres)

over 4000
2000-4000
1000-2000
400-1000
200-400
0-200
sea level
below sea level

Key to map symbols

◼ Over 5,000,000 inhabitants

● 1,000,000 - 5,000,000 inhabitants

• Under 1,000,000 inhabitants

Mexico Capital cities underlined

Country boundaries

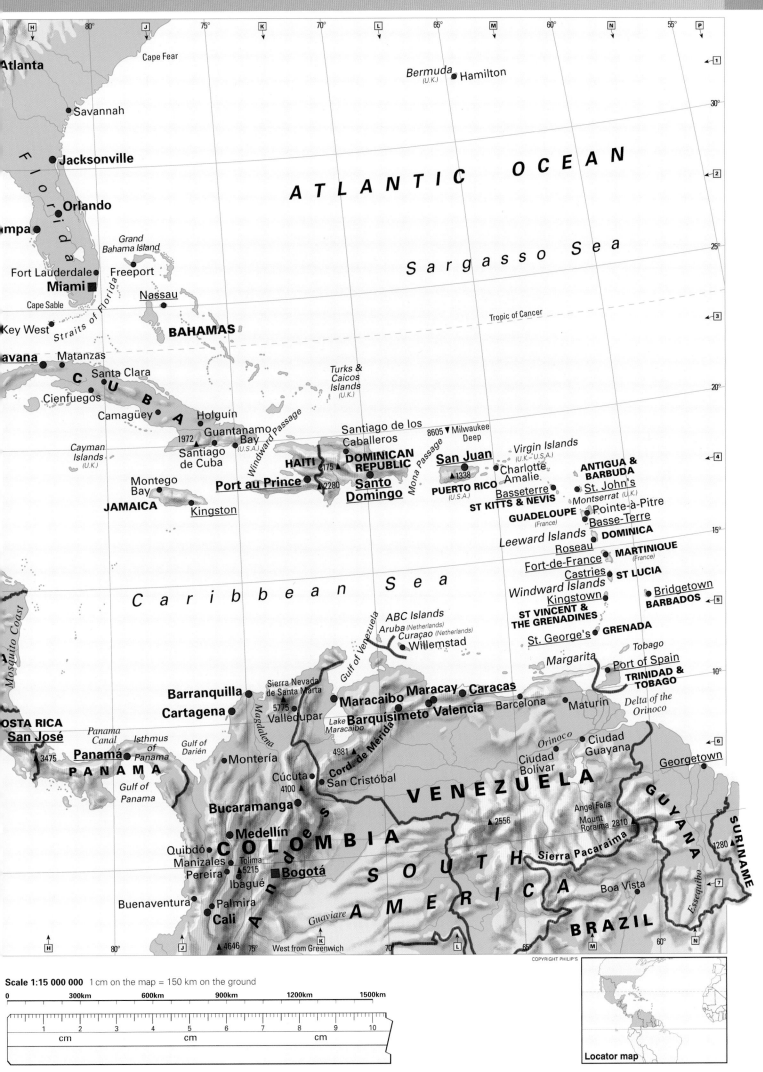

H 80° **J** 75° **K** 70° **L** 65° **M** 60° **N** 55° **P**

Atlanta

Cape Fear

Bermuda
(U.K.) ● Hamilton

1

30°

● Savannah

A T L A N T I C   O C E A N

● Jacksonville

2

● Orlando

F
l
o
r
i
d
a

ampa

S a r g a s s o   S e a

25°

Grand
Bahama Island

Fort Lauderdale ●   ● Freeport

Miami ■

Nassau

Cape Sable

Key West ●

Straits of Florida

BAHAMAS

Tropic of Cancer

3

avana   ● Matanzas

C

Santa Clara

● Cienfuegos

U

Turks &
Caicos
Islands
(U.K.)

20°

Camagüey

B

Holguín

8605 ▼ Milwaukee
Deep

Virgin Islands
(U.K.–U.S.A.)

**ANTIGUA &
BARBUDA**

1972 ▲

Guantanamo
Bay
(U.S.A.)

Santiago
de Cuba

A

Santiago de los
Caballeros

**DOMINICAN
REPUBLIC**

175 ▲

San Juan

▲1338

Charlotte
Amalie

4

*Cayman
Islands
(U.K.)*

HAITI

Port au Prince

▲2280

**Santo
Domingo**

PUERTO RICO
(U.S.A.)

Basseterre ●   ● **St. John's**

ST KITTS & NEVIS   Montserrat *(U.K.)*

Montego
Bay

● Kingston

JAMAICA

Mona Passage

Windward Passage

GUADELOUPE
(France)

● Pointe-à-Pitre

● **Basse-Terre**

DOMINICA

Leeward Islands

Roseau ●

MARTINIQUE
(France)

15°

Fort-de-France ●

C a r i b b e a n   S e a

Castries ●   **ST LUCIA**

Windward Islands

● **Bridgetown**

Kingstown ●

BARBADOS

5

**ST VINCENT &
THE GRENADINES**

Mosquito Coast

ABC Islands

Aruba *(Netherlands)*

Curaçao *(Netherlands)*

● Willemstad

St. George's ●   **GRENADA**

Tobago

Margarita

● Port of Spain

**TRINIDAD &
TOBAGO**

10°

● Barranquilla

Sierra Nevada
de Santa Marta

Gulf of Venezuela

Maracay

Maracaibo ●   ● Maracay   ● **Caracas**

● Barcelona

● Maturín

*Delta of the
Orinoco*

● Cartagena

5775 ▲

Magdalena

Valledupar

Lake
Maracaibo

Barquisimeto Valencia

COSTA RICA

San José

*Panama
Canal*

*Isthmus
of
Panama*

Gulf of Darién

4981 ▲

Cord. de Mérida

Orinoco

● Ciudad
Bolívar

● Ciudad
Guayana

6

▲3475

Panamá

PANAMA

*Gulf of
Panama*

● Montería

Cúcuta ●

4100 ▲

Cord.

● San Cristóbal

V E N E Z U E L A

● Georgetown

● Bucaramanga

Angel Falls

Mount
Roraima 2810

**G
U
Y
A
N
A**

1280

**S
U
R
I
N
A
M
E**

5°

● Medellín

Quibdó ●

Manizales ●

Pereira ●

Tolima
▲5215

Ibagué ●

COLOMBIA

▲2556

S
O
U
T
H

Sierra Pacaraima

Essequibo

● Boa Vista

7

A
n
d
e
s

■ **Bogotá**

A
M
E
R
I
C
A

Buenaventura ●

● Palmira

Cali ●

Guaviare

B
R
A
Z
I
L

H 80° **J** ▲4646 75° West from Greenwich 70° **L** 65° **M** 60° **N**

Scale 1:15 000 000   1 cm on the map = 150 km on the ground

0   300km   600km   900km   1200km   1500km

cm   cm   cm

COPYRIGHT PHILIP'S

Locator map

ATLANTIC OCEAN

CENTRAL AMERICA

Caribbean Sea

Greater Antilles

Leeward Islands

Lesser Antilles

Windward Islands

Panama Canal

Gulf of Panama

Magdalena

5775

Lake Maracaibo

Orinoco

Guiana Highlands

Angel Falls

Pico de Neblina
3014

Negro

Cotopaxi
5897

Chimborazo
6267

Japurá

Amazon Basin

Amazon

Amazon

Tocantins

Equator

Galapagos Islands

Ucayali

Selvas

Purus

Madeira

Tapajós

Xingu

Huascarán
6768

A n d e s

Lake Titicaca

Altiplano

Lake Poopó

Plateau of Mato Grosso

São Francisco

Brazilian Highlands

2890

Atacama Desert

Gran Chaco

Paraguay

Paraná

Iguaçu Falls

Ojos del Salado
6863

PACIFIC OCEAN

Tropic of Capricorn

Aconcagua
6962

Colorado

Paraná

Uruguay

Río de la Plata

Pampas

A n d e s

ATLANTIC OCEAN

Isla de Chiloé

Patagonia

Lago del Carbon
-105

Strait of Magellan

Tierra del Fuego

Falkland Islands

South Georgia

Cape Horn

110° West from Greenwich 100°

COPYRIGHT PHILIP'S

Height of the land (metres)

over 4000
3000 – 4000
2000 – 3000
1000 – 2000
500 – 1000
200 – 500
0 – 200
below sea level

sea level

Cross-section along latitude 20°S

CHILE   BOLIVIA   PARAGUAY   BRAZIL

▲ Ojos del Salado 6863
▲ Ancohuma & Illampu 6550

Pacific Ocean   Andes   Pilcomayo   Gran Chaco   Paraguay   Verde   Paraná   Brazilian Highlands   São Francisco   Doce   Atlantic Ocean

Pilcomayo

20°S   20°S

Scale 1:35 000 000

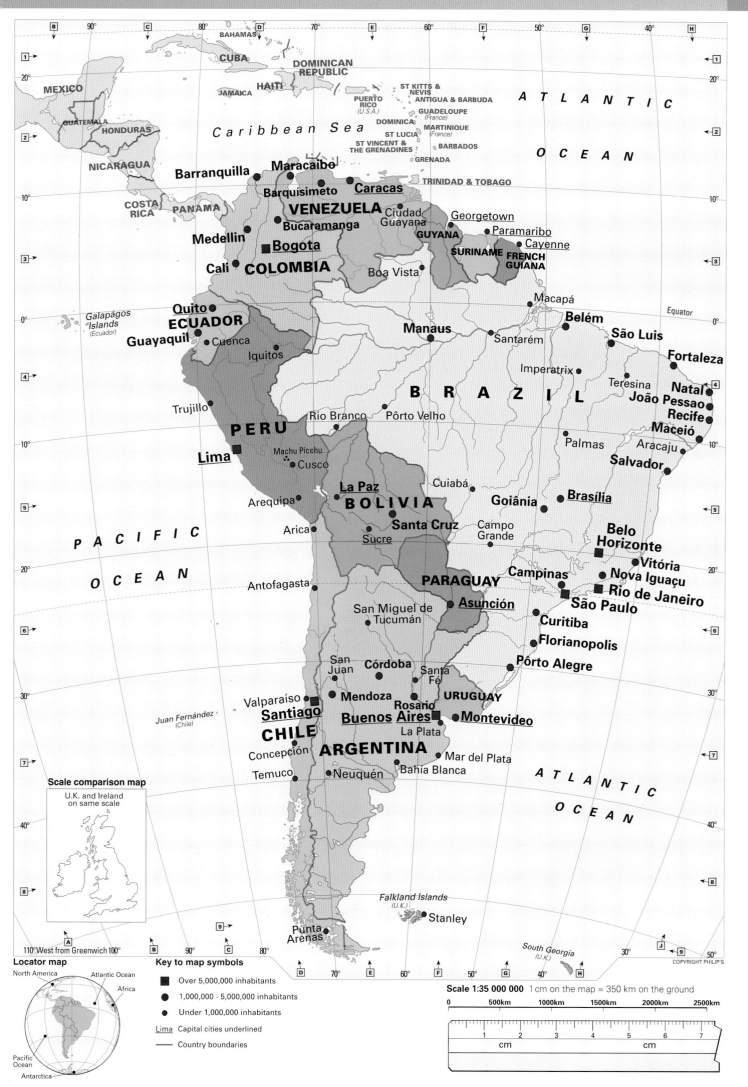

BAHAMAS
CUBA
DOMINICAN REPUBLIC
MEXICO
JAMAICA HAITI
PUERTO RICO (U.S.A.)
ST KITTS & NEVIS
ANTIGUA & BARBUDA
GUADELOUPE (France)
DOMINICA
ST LUCIA
MARTINIQUE (France)
BARBADOS
ST VINCENT & THE GRENADINES
GRENADA

GUATEMALA
HONDURAS
NICARAGUA
COSTA RICA
PANAMA

Caribbean Sea

ATLANTIC OCEAN

TRINIDAD & TOBAGO

Barranquilla
Maracaibo
Barquisimeto
Caracas
VENEZUELA
Ciudad Guayana
Georgetown
Bucaramanga
Medellin
Bogota
Cali
COLOMBIA
Boa Vista
GUYANA
Paramaribo
Cayenne
SURINAME
FRENCH GUIANA

Galápagos Islands (Ecuador)
Quito
ECUADOR
Guayaquil
Cuenca
Iquitos
Macapá
Belém
São Luis
Manaus
Santarém
Fortaleza
Equator

Trujillo
Rio Branco
Pôrto Velho
Imperatrix
Teresina
Natal
João Pessao
Recife
Maceió
Aracaju

PERU
B R A Z I L
Palmas

Lima
Machu Picchu
Cusco
Salvador

La Paz
Cuiabá
Goiânia
Brasília
Arequipa
BOLIVIA
Santa Cruz
Campo Grande
Belo Horizonte
Arica
Sucre
Vitória
Nova Iguaçu
Rio de Janeiro
PACIFIC OCEAN
Antofagasta
PARAGUAY
Campinas
São Paulo
Asunción
Curitiba
San Miguel de Tucumán
Florianopolis
Pôrto Alegre
San Juan
Córdoba
Santa Fé
URUGUAY
Valparaíso
Mendoza
Rosario
Juan Fernández (Chile)
Santiago
Buenos Aires
Montevideo
CHILE
La Plata
Concepción
ARGENTINA
Mar del Plata
Temuco
Neuquén
Bahía Blanca
ATLANTIC OCEAN

Falkland Islands (U.K.)
Stanley
Punta Arenas
South Georgia (U.K.)

110° West from Greenwich 100°
COPYRIGHT PHILIP'S

Scale comparison map
U.K. and Ireland on same scale

Locator map
North America
Atlantic Ocean
Africa
Pacific Ocean
Antarctica

Key to map symbols
■ Over 5,000,000 inhabitants
● 1,000,000 - 5,000,000 inhabitants
• Under 1,000,000 inhabitants
Lima Capital cities underlined
---- Country boundaries

Scale 1:35 000 000   1 cm on the map = 350 km on the ground
0   500km   1000km   1500km   2000km   2500km

cm   cm

Locator map

Scale 1:21 000 000   1 cm on the map = 210 km on the ground

0   210km   420km   630km   840km   1050km   1260km

cm

Height of the land (metres)

over 4000
2000 – 4000
1000 – 2000
400 – 1000
200 – 400
0 – 200
sea level
below sea level

Key to map symbols

■ Over 5,000,000 inhabitants
● 1,000,000 – 5,000,000 inhabitants
• Under 1,000,000 inhabitants

Brasília   Capital cities underlined

Country boundaries

State boundaries

WEALTH

The value of total production divided by the population in US$ 2010

Over $10,000
$7,500 – 10,000
$5,000 – 7,500
Under $5,000

COPYRIGHT PHILIP'S

POPULATION DENSITY

The number of people per square kilometre

Over 100
50 – 100
10 – 50
Under 10

The Arctic

Height of the land (metres)

- over 4000
- 2000-4000
- 1000-2000
- 400-1000
- 200-400
- 0-200 (sea level)
- below sea level

Yukon
Alaska (U.S.A.)
Cape Barrow
Wrangel Island (Russia)
Nizhne Kolymsk
Mackenzie
Inuvik
Prudhoe Bay
Beaufort Sea
East Siberian Sea
New Siberian Islands (Russia)
Tiksi
Laptev Sea
Lena
Siberia

NORTH
Great Bear Lake
ARCTIC OCEAN

Yellowknife
Great Slave Lake
AMERICA
Banks Island (Canada)
North Magnetic Pole + 2007
Cape Chelyuskin
Taimyr Peninsula
RUSSIA

Churchill
Victoria Island (Canada)
Queen Elizabeth Islands (Canada)
North Pole
Severnaya Zemlya (Russia)
Norilsk
Yenisey

CANADA
Arctic Circle
Ellesmere Island (Canada)
Nares Strait
Lincoln Sea
Cape Morris Jessup
80°N
Franz Josef Land (Russia)
Novaya Zemlya (Russia)
Kara Sea
Gulf of Ob
Surgut

Hudson Bay
Parry Channel
Baffin Island (Canada)
Baffin Bay
McKinley Sea
Vorkuta
Ob

Iqaluit
Hudson Strait
Davis Strait
Longyearbyen
Svalbard (Norway)
Barents Sea
Ural Mountains

Labrador
Greenland (Denmark)
Greenland Sea
Bear Island (Norway)
Murmansk

Nuuk
Mont Forel 3360
3700
Jan Mayen Island (Norway)
North Cape
White Sea
Arkhangelsk
Northern Dvina

Cape Farewell
Denmark Strait
70°N
Tromsø
NORWAY
FINLAND

20° West from Greenwich 0° East from Greenwich 20° 40°

Antarctica

Scotia Sea
West from Greenwich
East from Greenwich

Stanley
Falkland Islands (U.K.)
South Orkney Islands
Antarctic Circle
Sanae (South Africa)
Lazarev Sea
Riiser-Larsen Sea
SOUTHERN OCEAN

Tierra del Fuego
Drake Passage
Cape Horn
O'Higgins (Chile)
Esperanza (Argentina)
Weddell Sea
Brunt Ice Shelf
Queen Maud Land
Cosmonaut Sea

CHILE
Punta Arenas
Palmer (U.S.A.)
South Shetland Islands
Antarctic Peninsula
Halley (U.K.)
Coats Land
Enderby Land
Kemp Land

Anvers Island
Larsen Ice Shelf
80°S
MacRobertson Land
Mawson (Australia)

Adelaide Island
Rothera (U.K.)
Palmer Land
Berkner Island
Prince Charles Mountains
Amery Ice Shelf
Cape Darnley

Wilkins Ice Shelf
Ronne Ice Shelf
Lambert Glacier
Prydz Bay

Alexander Island
Bellinghausen Sea
Ellsworth Land
Queen Elizabeth Land
American Highland
Davis (Australia)

Peter I Island
Ellsworth Mountains
Patriot Hills (Chile)
Vinson Massif 4897
South Pole
Amundsen-Scott (U.S.A.)
East Antarctica
Queen Mary Land
Davis Sea

Thurston Island
West Antarctica
Queen Maud Mountains
Vostok (Russia)
Shackleton Ice Shelf

Marie Byrd Land
Beardmore Glacier
Transantarctic Mountains
Mount Markham 4349
Wilkes Land

Amundsen Sea
Ross Ice Shelf
Casey (Australia)
Antarctic Circle

Scott (N.Z.)
Mount Erebus 3743
McMurdo (U.S.A.)
Victoria Land

Ross Sea
Adélie Land
Dumont d'Urville (France)

Cape Adare
South Magnetic Pole + 2007
Oates Land

COPYRIGHT PHILIP'S

Key to map symbols

- Height of ice (in metres)
- Land permanently covered with ice
- Land over 3000 metres
- ● Permanent settlements
- Nuuk Capital cities underlined
- Davis (Australia) Selected research station and the country which runs it

Scale 1:35 000 000 1 cm on the map = 350 km on the ground

0 500km 1000km 1500km 2000km 2500km 3000km

1 2 3 4 5 6 7 8
cm cm

Scale comparison map

U.K. and Ireland on same scale

CONTINENT	AREA '000 kilometres	COLDEST PLACE degrees Celsius		HOTTEST PLACE degrees Celsius		WETTEST PLACE average annual rainfall, mm		DRIEST PLACE average annual rainfall,
Asia	44,500	Oymyakon, Russia −70°C	①	Tirat Zevi, Israel 54°C	⑧	Mawsynram, India 11,870	⑮	Aden, Yemen 46
Africa	30,302	Ifrane, Morocco −24°C	②	Al Aziziyah, Libya 58°C	⑨	Debundscha, Cameroon 10,290	⑯	Wadi Haifa, Sudan 2
North America	24,241	Snag, Yukon −63°C	③	Death Valley, California 57°C	⑩	Henderson Lake, Canada 6,500	⑰	Bataques, Mexico 30
South America	17,793	Sarmiento, Argentina −33°C	④	Rivadavia, Argentina 49°C	⑪	Quibdó, Colombia 8,990	⑱	Quillagua, Chile 0.6
Antarctica	14,000	Vostok −89°C	⑤	Vanda Station 15°C	⑫			
Europe	9,957	Ust Shchugor, Russia −55°C	⑥	Seville, Spain 50°C	⑬	Crkvice, Montenegro 4,650	⑲	Astrakhan, Russia 160
Oceania	8,557	Charlotte Pass, Australia −22°C	⑦	Oodnadatta, Australia 51°C	⑭	Tully, Australia 4,550	⑳	Mulka, Australia 100

Equatorial Scale 1:95 000 000
1 cm on the map = 950 km on the ground

Height of the land (metres)

over 6000
4000 – 6000
2000 – 4000
1000 – 2000
200 – 1000
0 – 200
below sea level

COPYRIGHT PHILIP'S

LARGEST SEAS '000 square kilometres		LARGEST LAKES '000 square kilometres		LONGEST RIVERS kilometres		LARGEST ISLANDS '000 square kilometres		HIGHEST PEAKS metres		DEEPEST TRENCHES metres	
Pacific Ocean 155,557	(27)	Caspian Sea 371	(37)	Nile 6,695	(47)	Greenland 2,176	(57)	Himalayas: Mount Everest 8,850	(67)	Mariana Trench 11,022	(77)
Atlantic Ocean 76,762	(28)	Lake Superior 82	(38)	Amazon 6,450	(48)	New Guinea 821	(58)	Karakoram: K2 8,611	(68)	Tonga Trench 10,822	(78)
Indian Ocean 68,556	(29)	Lake Victoria 68	(39)	Yangtse 6,380	(49)	Borneo 744	(59)	Pamirs: Ismail Samani Peak 7,495	(69)	Japan Trench 10,554	(79)
Southern Ocean 20,237	(30)	Lake Huron 60	(40)	Mississippi-Missouri 5,971	(50)	Madagascar 587	(60)	Tian Shan: Pobedy Peak 7,439	(70)	Kuril Trench 10,542	(80)
Arctic Ocean 14,351	(31)	Lake Michigan 58	(41)	Yenisey-Angara 5,550	(51)	Baffin Island 508	(61)	Andes: Aconcagua 6,962	(71)	Mindanao Trench 10,497	(81)
Mediterranean Sea 2,966	(32)	Lake Tanganyika 33	(42)	Hwang-Ho 5,464	(52)	Sumatra 474	(62)	Rocky Mountains: Mount McKinley 6,194	(72)	Kermadec Trench 10,047	(82)
South China Sea 2,318	(33)	Great Bear Lake 32	(43)	Ob-Irtysh 5,410	(53)	Honshu 231	(63)	East Africa: Kilimanjaro 5,895	(73)	Bougainville Trench 9,140	(83)
Bering Sea 2,274	(34)	Lake Baikal 31	(44)	Congo 4,670	(54)	Great Britain 230	(64)	Caucasus: Elbrus 5,642	(74)	Milwaukee Deep 8,605	(84)
Caribbean Sea 1,942	(35)	Lake Malawi 30	(45)	Mekong 4,500	(55)	Victoria Island 212	(65)	Antarctica: Vinson Massif 4,897	(75)	South Sandwich Trench 7,235	(85)
Gulf of Mexico 1,813	(36)	Great Slave Lake 29	(46)	Amur 4,442	(56)	Ellesmere Island 197	(66)	Alps: Mont Blanc 4,808	(76)	Aleutian Trench 7,822	(86)

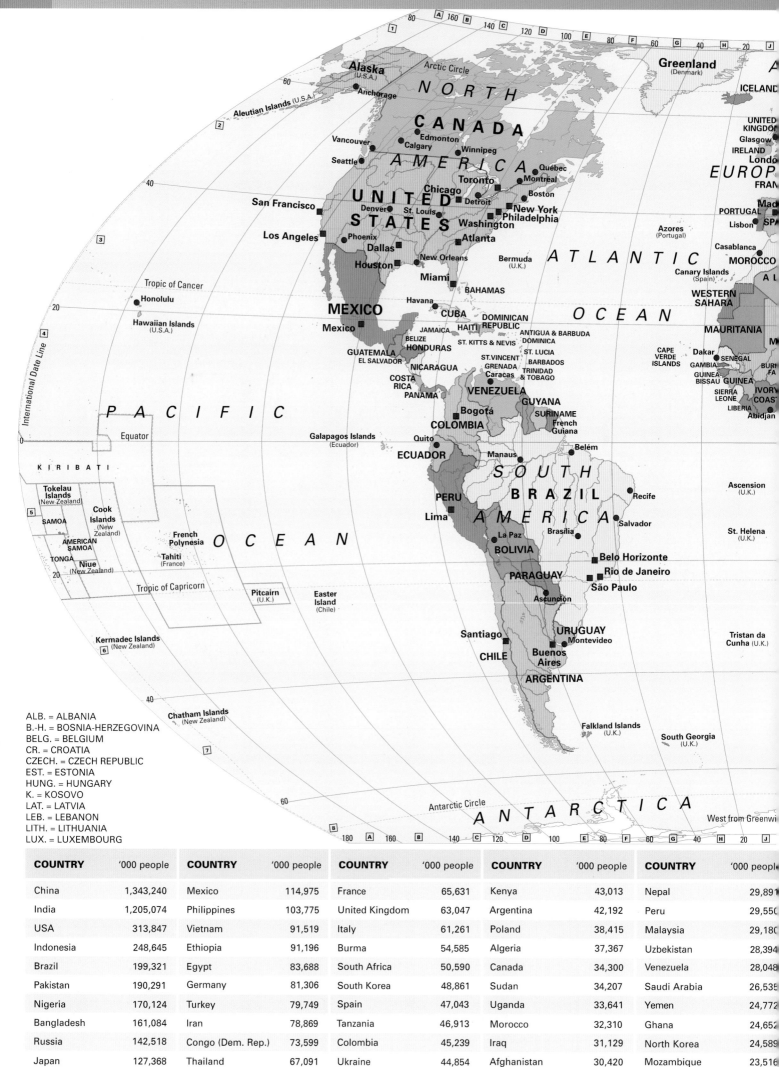

ALB. = ALBANIA
B.-H. = BOSNIA-HERZEGOVINA
BELG. = BELGIUM
CR. = CROATIA
CZECH. = CZECH REPUBLIC
EST. = ESTONIA
HUNG. = HUNGARY
K. = KOSOVO
LAT. = LATVIA
LEB. = LEBANON
LITH. = LITHUANIA
LUX. = LUXEMBOURG

COUNTRY	'000 people	COUNTRY	'000 people	COUNTRY	'000 people	COUNTRY	'000 people	COUNTRY	'000 people
China	1,343,240	Mexico	114,975	France	65,631	Kenya	43,013	Nepal	29,891
India	1,205,074	Philippines	103,775	United Kingdom	63,047	Argentina	42,192	Peru	29,550
USA	313,847	Vietnam	91,519	Italy	61,261	Poland	38,415	Malaysia	29,180
Indonesia	248,645	Ethiopia	91,196	Burma	54,585	Algeria	37,367	Uzbekistan	28,394
Brazil	199,321	Egypt	83,688	South Africa	50,590	Canada	34,300	Venezuela	28,048
Pakistan	190,291	Germany	81,306	South Korea	48,861	Sudan	34,207	Saudi Arabia	26,535
Nigeria	170,124	Turkey	79,749	Spain	47,043	Uganda	33,641	Yemen	24,772
Bangladesh	161,084	Iran	78,869	Tanzania	46,913	Morocco	32,310	Ghana	24,652
Russia	142,518	Congo (Dem. Rep.)	73,599	Colombia	45,239	Iraq	31,129	North Korea	24,589
Japan	127,368	Thailand	67,091	Ukraine	44,854	Afghanistan	30,420	Mozambique	23,516

Equatorial Scale 1:95 000 000
1 cm on the map = 950 km on the ground

M. = MONTENEGRO
MACED. = MACEDONIA
MOLD. = MOLDOVA
NETH.= NETHERLANDS
SERB. = SERBIA
SLO. = SLOVENIA
SLOV. = SLOVAK REPUBLIC
SWITZ. = SWITZERLAND
U.A.E. = UNITED ARAB EMIRATES
U.K. = UNITED KINGDOM
U.S.A = UNITED STATES OF AMERICA

COUNTRY	'000 people	COUNTRY	'000 people	COUNTRY	'000 people	COUNTRY	'000 people	COUNTRY	'000 people
Taiwan	23,235	Burkina Faso	17,275	Senegal	12,970	Burundi	10,557	Azerbaijan	9,494
Syria	22,531	Chile	17,067	Zimbabwe	12,620	Belgium	10,438	Sweden	9,104
Australia	22,016	Netherlands	16,731	Rwanda	11,690	Bolivia	10,290	Honduras	8,297
Madagascar	22,005	Niger	16,345	Cuba	11,075	Czech Republic	10,177	Austria	8,220
Ivory Coast	21,952	Malawi	16,323	Chad	10,976	Dominican Republic	10,089	Switzerland	7,926
Romania	21,849	Mali	15,494	Guinea	10,885	Somalia	10,086	Tajikistan	7,768
Sri Lanka	21,481	Ecuador	15,224	Portugal	10,781	Hungary	9,958	Israel	7,591
Cameroon	20,130	Cambodia	14,953	Greece	10,768	Haiti	9,802	Serbia	7,277
Angola	18,056	Guatemala	14,099	Tunisia	10,733	Belarus	8,644	Bulgaria	7,038
Kazakhstan	17,522	Zambia	13,817	South Sudan	10,625	Benin	8,599	Togo	6,961

COPYRIGHT PHILIP'S

CLIMATE REGIONS

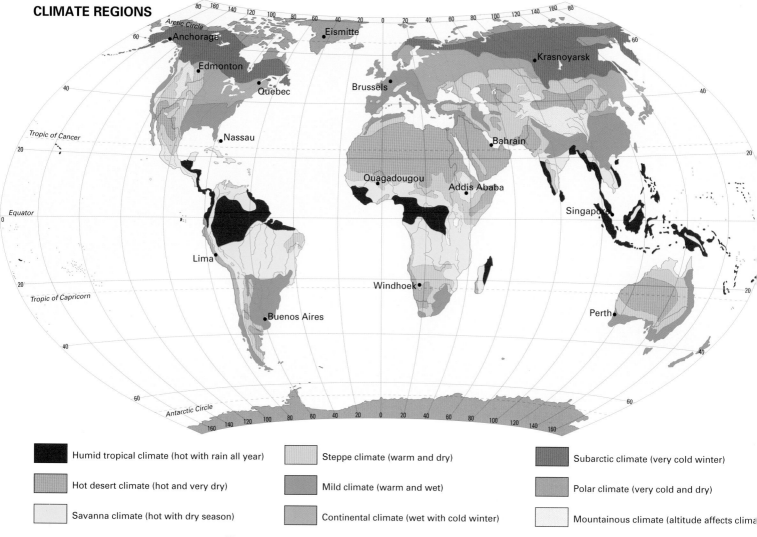

The map shows how the world can be divided into 9 broad climate regions.

Legend:

- Humid tropical climate (hot with rain all year)
- Hot desert climate (hot and very dry)
- Savanna climate (hot with dry season)
- Steppe climate (warm and dry)
- Mild climate (warm and wet)
- Continental climate (wet with cold winter)
- Subarctic climate (very cold winter)
- Polar climate (very cold and dry)
- Mountainous climate (altitude affects clima...

CLIMATE GRAPHS

The graphs below give examples of places within each climate region, showing how temperature and rainfall vary from month to month.

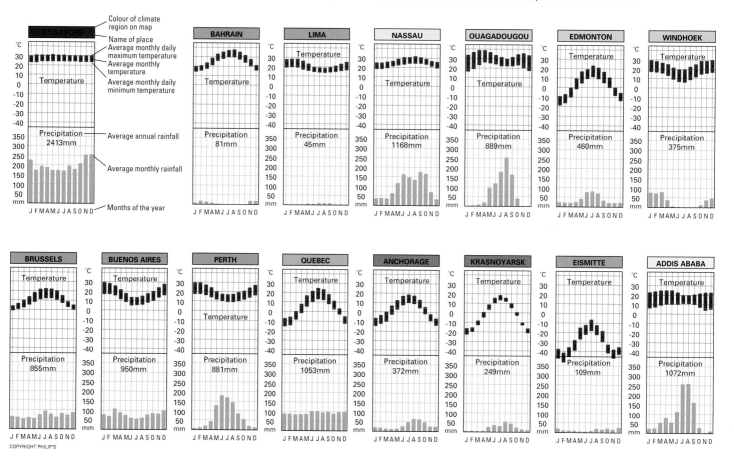

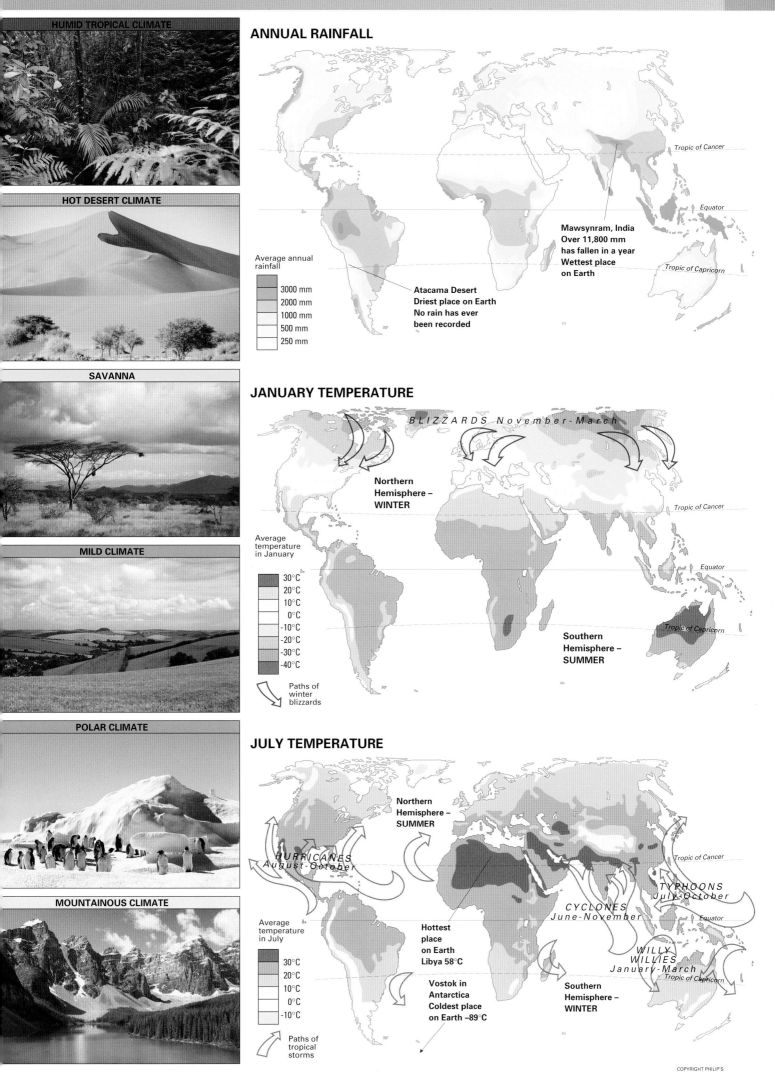

HUMID TROPICAL CLIMATE

HOT DESERT CLIMATE

SAVANNA

MILD CLIMATE

POLAR CLIMATE

MOUNTAINOUS CLIMATE

ANNUAL RAINFALL

Tropic of Cancer

Equator

Mawsynram, India
Over 11,800 mm
has fallen in a year
Wettest place
on Earth

Tropic of Capricorn

Average annual
rainfall

- 3000 mm
- 2000 mm
- 1000 mm
- 500 mm
- 250 mm

Atacama Desert
Driest place on Earth
No rain has ever
been recorded

JANUARY TEMPERATURE

BLIZZARDS November–March

Northern
Hemisphere –
WINTER

Tropic of Cancer

Average
temperature
in January

- 30°C
- 20°C
- 10°C
- 0°C
- -10°C
- -20°C
- -30°C
- -40°C

Equator

Tropic of Capricorn

Southern
Hemisphere –
SUMMER

Paths of
winter
blizzards

JULY TEMPERATURE

Northern
Hemisphere –
SUMMER

HURRICANES
August–October

Tropic of Cancer

TYPHOONS
July–October

CYCLONES
June–November

Equator

WILLY
WILLIES
January–March

Tropic of Capricorn

Average
temperature
in July

- 30°C
- 20°C
- 10°C
- 0°C
- -10°C

Hottest
place
on Earth
Libya 58°C

Vostok in
Antarctica
Coldest place
on Earth –89°C

Southern
Hemisphere –
WINTER

Paths of
tropical
storms

COPYRIGHT PHILIP'S

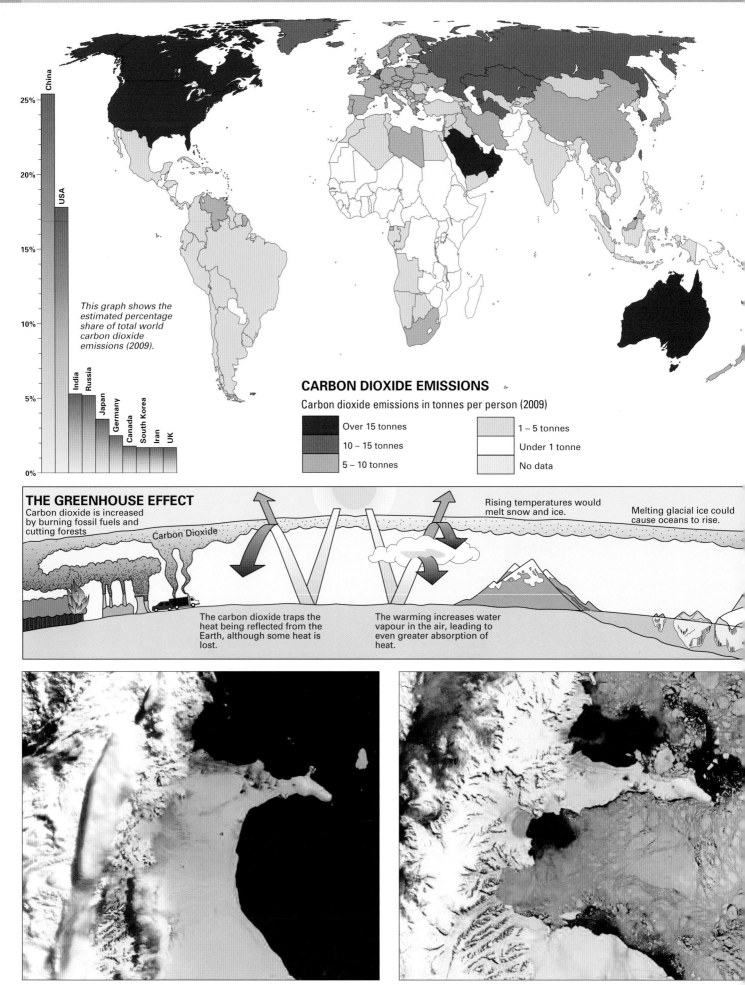

This graph shows the estimated percentage share of total world carbon dioxide emissions (2009).

China
USA
India
Russia
Japan
Germany
Canada
South Korea
Iran
UK

25%
20%
15%
10%
5%
0%

CARBON DIOXIDE EMISSIONS

Carbon dioxide emissions in tonnes per person (2009)

Over 15 tonnes	1 – 5 tonnes
10 – 15 tonnes	Under 1 tonne
5 – 10 tonnes	No data

THE GREENHOUSE EFFECT

Carbon dioxide is increased by burning fossil fuels and cutting forests

Carbon Dioxide

Rising temperatures would melt snow and ice.

Melting glacial ice could cause oceans to rise.

The carbon dioxide traps the heat being reflected from the Earth, although some heat is lost.

The warming increases water vapour in the air, leading to even greater absorption of heat.

▲ Larsen B ice shelf, Antarctica. Between January and March 2002, Larsen B ice shelf on the Antarctic Peninsula collapsed. The image on the left shows its area before the collapse, while the image on the right shows the area after the collapse. The 200 m thick ice sheet had been retreating before this date, but over 500 billion tonnes of ice collapsed in under a month. This was due to rising temperatures of 0.5°C per year in this part of Antarctica. Satellite images like these a the only way for scientists to monitor inaccessible areas of the worl

COPYRIGHT PHILIP'S

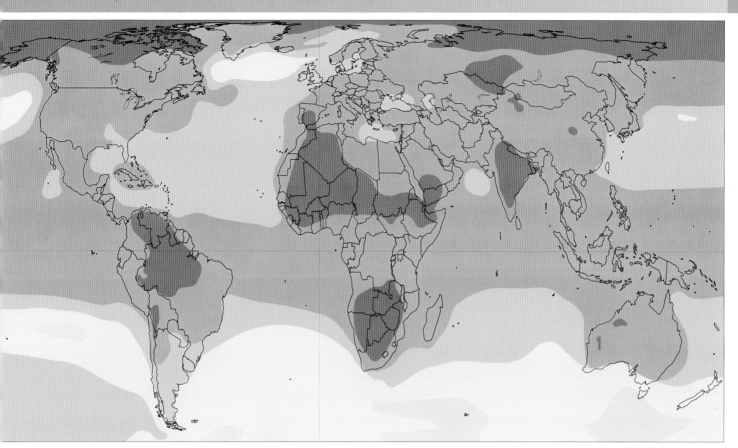

EDICTED CHANGE IN TEMPERATURE

e difference between actual annual
rage surface air temperature, 1969–1990,
d predicted annual average surface
temperature, 2070–2100

▓ 5 – 10°C warmer	░ 1 – 2°C warmer
▒ 3 – 5°C warmer	░ 0 – 1°C warmer
▒ 2 – 3°C warmer	

*These maps shows the predicted
increase assuming a 'medium growth'
of the global economy and assuming
that no measures to combat the
emission of greenhouse gases
are taken.*

*It should be noted that these predicted
annual average changes mask quite
significant seasonal detail.*

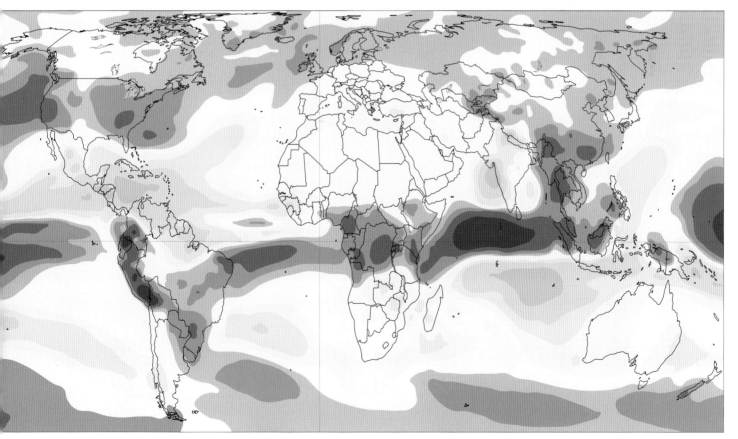

EDICTED CHANGE IN RAINFALL

e difference between actual annual average
fall, 1969–1990, and predicted annual
rage rainfall, 2070–2100

Over 2 mm more rain per day	0.2 – 0.5 mm more rain per day	0.5 – 1 mm less rain per day
1 – 2 mm more rain per day	No change	1 – 2 mm less rain per day
Over 2 mm more rain per day	0.2 – 0.5 mm less rain per day	Over 2 mm less rain per day

*ce: The Hadley Centre of Climate Prediction
Research, Met Office*

COPYRIGHT PHILIP'S

TUNDRA AND MOUNTAIN VEGETATION

NEEDLELEAF EVERGREEN FOREST

MID-LATITUDE GRASSLAND

TROPICAL BROADLEAF RAINFOREST

DESERT

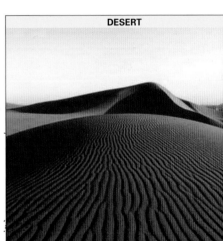

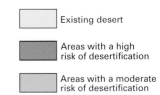

Desertification is the process by which a desert gradually spreads into neighbouring areas of semi-desert. It is usually the result of human activity, such as overgrazing by livestock.

DESERTIFICATION

Existing desert

Areas with a high risk of desertification

Areas with a moderate risk of desertification

COPYRIGHT PHILIP'S

NATURAL VEGETATION

The map shows the type of vegetation that would grow if people were not there. People have cleared forests and natural grasslands for thousands of years. Most of the broadleaf deciduous woodland that would naturally cover Britain and Ireland has been cleared for farming and for building. In more recent years, much of the tropical broadleaf rainforest and monsoon forests have been felled.

Tundra and mountain vegetation

Needleleaf evergreen forest

Mixed forest of needleleaf evergreen and broadleaf deciduous trees

Broadleaf deciduous woodland

Mid-latitude grassland

Evergreen broadleaf and deciduous trees, shrubs and herbs

Semi-desert scrub

Desert

Tropical grassland (savanna)

Tropical broadleaf rainforest and needleleaf forest

Sub-tropical broadleaf and needleleaf forest

⸱EFORESTATION

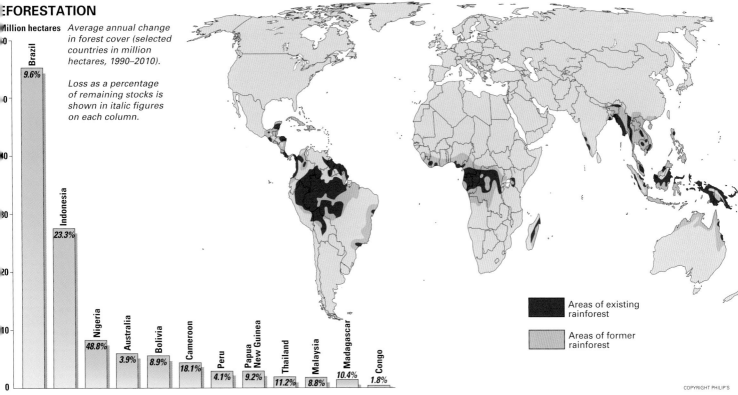

Million hectares

Average annual change in forest cover (selected countries in million hectares, 1990–2010).

Loss as a percentage of remaining stocks is shown in italic figures on each column.

- Brazil — 9.6%
- Indonesia — 23.3%
- Nigeria — 48.8%
- Australia — 3.9%
- Bolivia — 8.9%
- Cameroon — 18.1%
- Peru — 4.1%
- Papua New Guinea — 9.2%
- Thailand — 11.2%
- Malaysia — 8.8%
- Madagascar — 10.4%
- Congo — 1.8%

Areas of existing rainforest

Areas of former rainforest

COPYRIGHT PHILIP'S

CONTINENTAL DRIFT

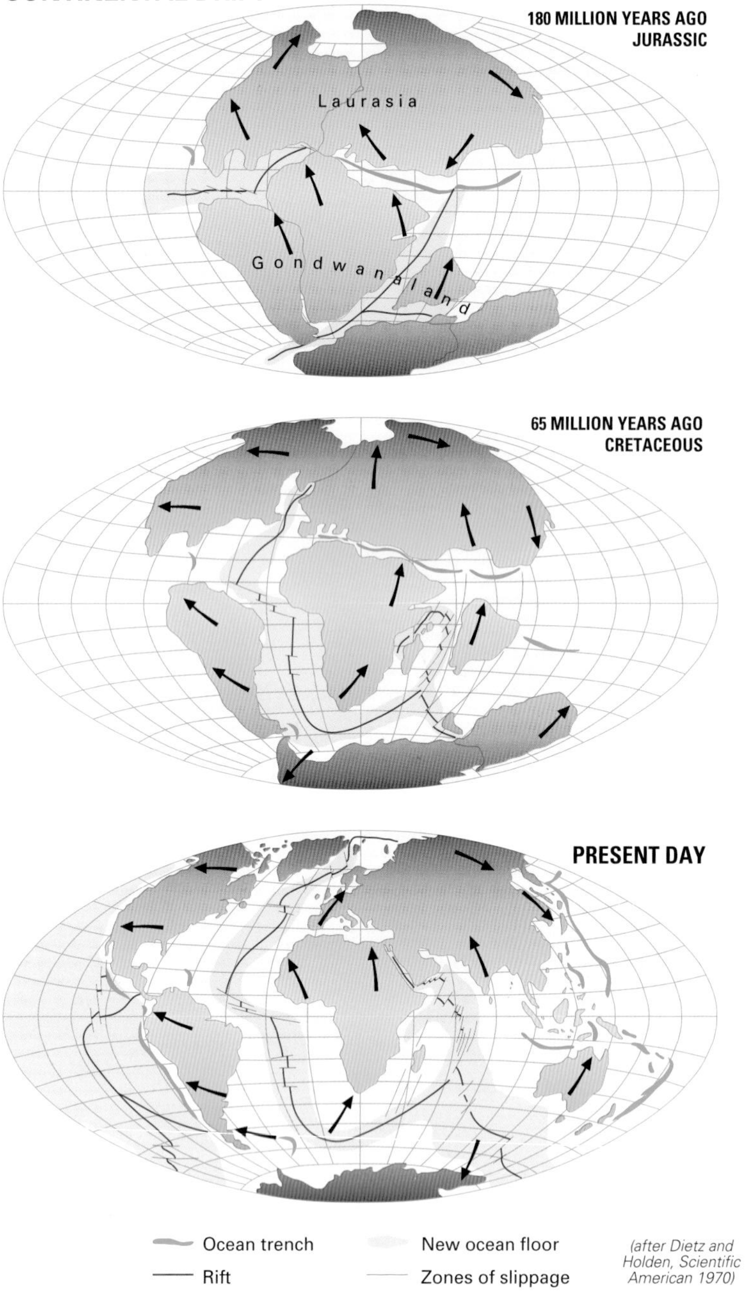
180 MILLION YEARS AGO
JURASSIC
Laurasia
Gondwanaland
65 MILLION YEARS AGO
CRETACEOUS
PRESENT DAY
Ocean trench
Rift
New ocean floor
Zones of slippage
(after Dietz and Holden, Scientific American 1970)

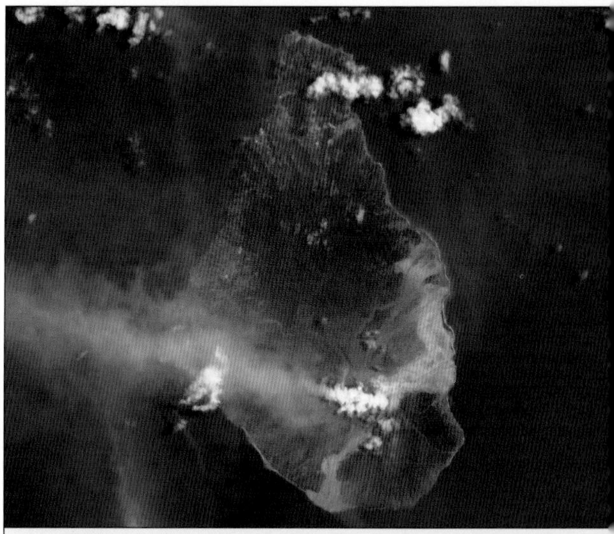

▲ In 1995, after almost 400 years lying dormant, the Soufrière Hills volcano on the Caribbean island of Montserrat began a series of eruptions. Further eruptions in 1996 and 1997 left the south of the island uninhabitable and 5,000 people had to be evacuated to the northern zone. Steam can be seen rising from the volcano in the false colour satellite image, above.

SOUFRIÈRE HILLS VOLCANO, MONTSERRAT

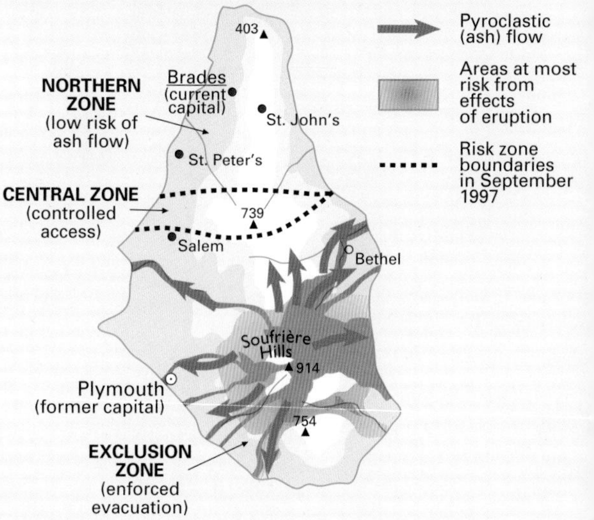
403
NORTHERN ZONE
(low risk of ash flow)
Brades
(current capital)
St. John's
St. Peter's
CENTRAL ZONE
(controlled access)
739
Salem
Bethel
Soufrière Hills
914
Plymouth
(former capital)
754
EXCLUSION ZONE
(enforced evacuation)
Pyroclastic (ash) flow
Areas at most risk from effects of eruption
Risk zone boundaries in September 1997

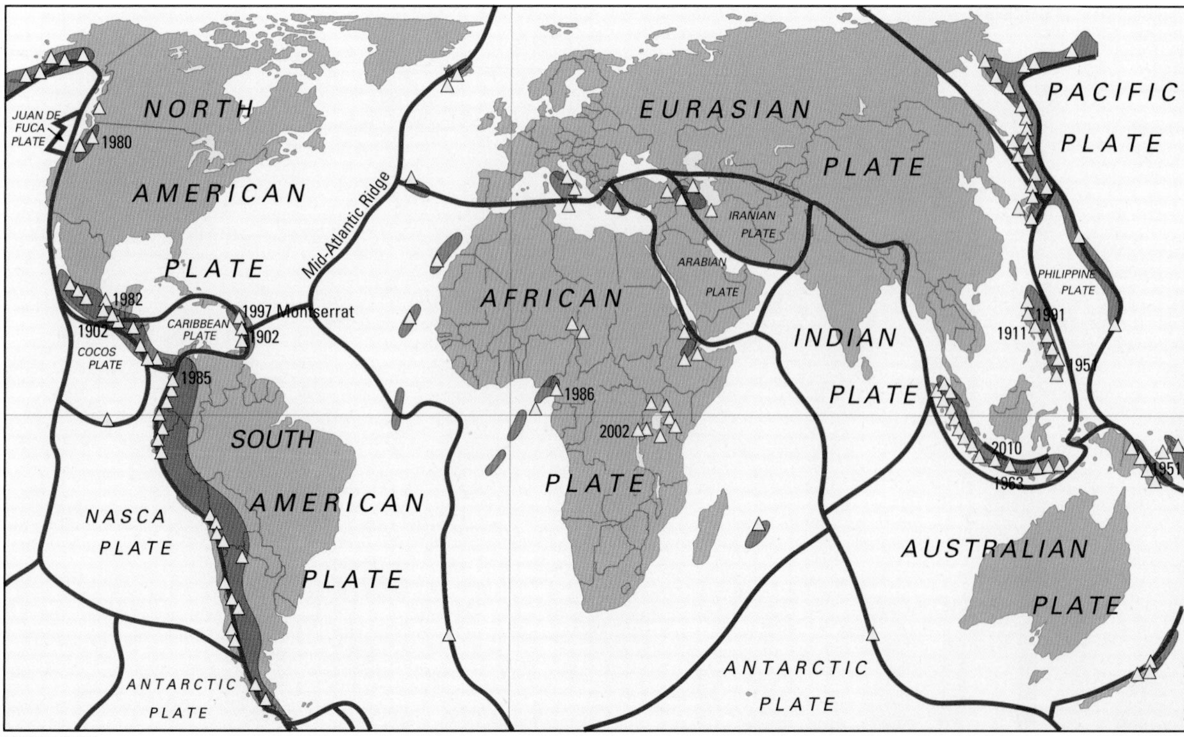
JUAN DE FUCA PLATE
1980
NORTH AMERICAN PLATE
Mid-Atlantic Ridge
EURASIAN PLATE
PACIFIC PLATE
IRANIAN PLATE
ARABIAN PLATE
AFRICAN PLATE
INDIAN PLATE
PHILIPPINE PLATE
1982
1997 Montserrat
CARIBBEAN PLATE
1902
1902
COCOS PLATE
1985
1986
2002
1911
1991
1951
2010
1963
1951
SOUTH AMERICAN PLATE
NASCA PLATE
AUSTRALIAN PLATE
ANTARCTIC PLATE
ANTARCTIC PLATE

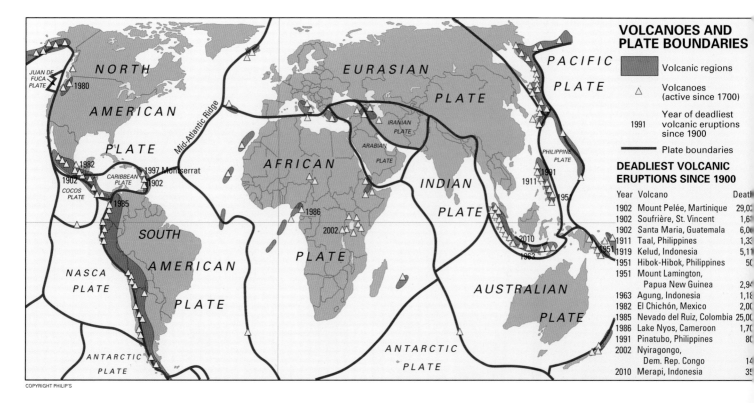

VOLCANOES AND PLATE BOUNDARIES

Volcanic regions
Volcanoes (active since 1700)
1991 Year of deadliest volcanic eruptions since 1900
Plate boundaries

DEADLIEST VOLCANIC ERUPTIONS SINCE 1900

Year	Volcano	Deat
1902	Mount Pelée, Martinique	29,0
1902	Soufrière, St. Vincent	1,6
1902	Santa Maria, Guatemala	6,0
1911	Taal, Philippines	1,3
1919	Kelud, Indonesia	5,11
1951	Hibok-Hibok, Philippines	5
1951	Mount Lamington, Papua New Guinea	2,9
1963	Agung, Indonesia	1,1
1982	El Chichón, Mexico	2,0
1985	Nevado del Ruiz, Colombia	25,0
1986	Lake Nyos, Cameroon	1,7
1991	Pinatubo, Philippines	8
2002	Nyiragongo, Dem. Rep. Congo	1
2010	Merapi, Indonesia	3

COPYRIGHT PHILIP'S

PLATE TECTONICS IN THE CARIBBEAN

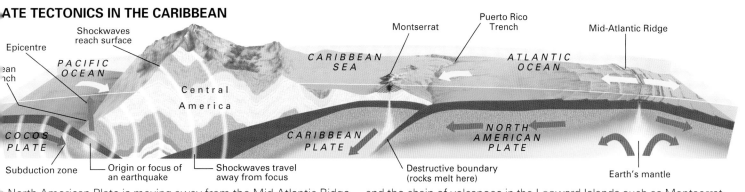

Epicentre — PACIFIC OCEAN — Shockwaves reach surface — Montserrat — Puerto Rico Trench — Mid-Atlantic Ridge — CARIBBEAN SEA — ATLANTIC OCEAN — Central America — NORTH AMERICAN PLATE — CARIBBEAN PLATE — COCOS PLATE — Subduction zone — Origin or focus of an earthquake — Shockwaves travel away from focus — Destructive boundary (rocks melt here) — Earth's mantle

The North American Plate is moving away from the Mid-Atlantic Ridge towards the Caribbean Plate at a rate of 30-40mm a year. The edge of the North American Plate is forced downwards under the Caribbean Plate. As the North American Plate descends, the rocks melt and are destroyed. This is called a *destructive boundary*. The destructive boundary to the east of the Caribbean has caused the Puerto Rico Trench

and the chain of volcanoes in the Leeward Islands such as Montserrat. The molten rocks along the destructive boundary are forced upwards through cracks at the edge of the Caribbean Plate to pour out as lava from volcanoes. Earthquakes are also common along destructive plate boundaries, as is the case in Central America, along the boundary between the Caribbean and Cocos Plates.

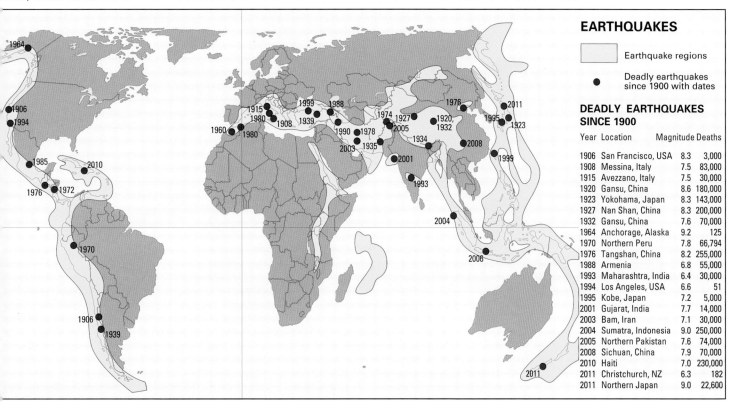

EARTHQUAKES

- Earthquake regions
- • Deadly earthquakes since 1900 with dates

DEADLY EARTHQUAKES SINCE 1900

Year	Location	Magnitude	Deaths
1906	San Francisco, USA	8.3	3,000
1908	Messina, Italy	7.5	83,000
1915	Avezzano, Italy	7.5	30,000
1920	Gansu, China	8.6	180,000
1923	Yokohama, Japan	8.3	143,000
1927	Nan Shan, China	8.3	200,000
1932	Gansu, China	7.6	70,000
1964	Anchorage, Alaska	9.2	125
1970	Northern Peru	7.8	66,794
1976	Tangshan, China	8.2	255,000
1988	Armenia	6.8	55,000
1993	Maharashtra, India	6.4	30,000
1994	Los Angeles, USA	6.6	51
1995	Kobe, Japan	7.2	5,000
2001	Gujarat, India	7.7	14,000
2003	Bam, Iran	7.1	30,000
2004	Sumatra, Indonesia	9.0	250,000
2005	Northern Pakistan	7.6	74,000
2008	Sichuan, China	7.9	70,000
2010	Haiti	7.0	230,000
2011	Christchurch, NZ	6.3	182
2011	Northern Japan	9.0	22,600

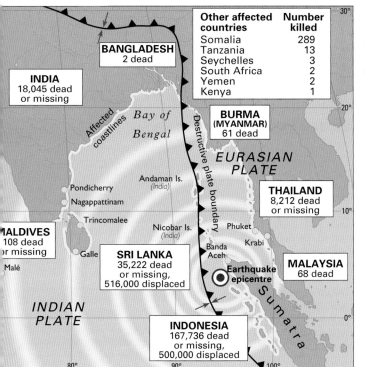

Other affected countries	Number killed
Somalia	289
Tanzania	13
Seychelles	3
South Africa	2
Yemen	2
Kenya	1

BANGLADESH 2 dead

INDIA 18,045 dead or missing

BURMA (MYANMAR) 61 dead

EURASIAN PLATE

Bay of Bengal

Affected coastlines

Destructive plate boundary

Andaman Is. (India)

THAILAND 8,212 dead or missing

Pondicherry
Nagappattinam
Trincomalee

Nicobar Is. (India)

Phuket

MALDIVES 108 dead or missing

Malé

Galle

SRI LANKA 35,222 dead or missing, 516,000 displaced

Krabi
Banda Aceh

Earthquake epicentre

MALAYSIA 68 dead

INDIAN PLATE

Sumatra

INDONESIA 167,736 dead or missing, 500,000 displaced

COPYRIGHT PHILIP'S

INDIAN OCEAN TSUNAMI

On 26 December 2004, an earthquake off the coast of Sumatra triggered a deadly tsunami that swept across the Indian Ocean, causing devastation in many countries (see map left).
The image below shows the turbulent receding waters of the tsunami, on the west coast of Sri Lanka. Such imagery enabled rescuers to assess the worst affected areas.

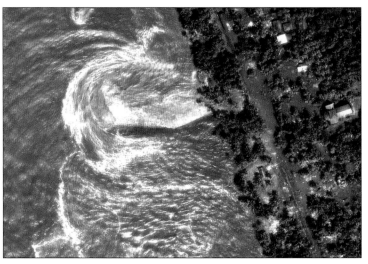

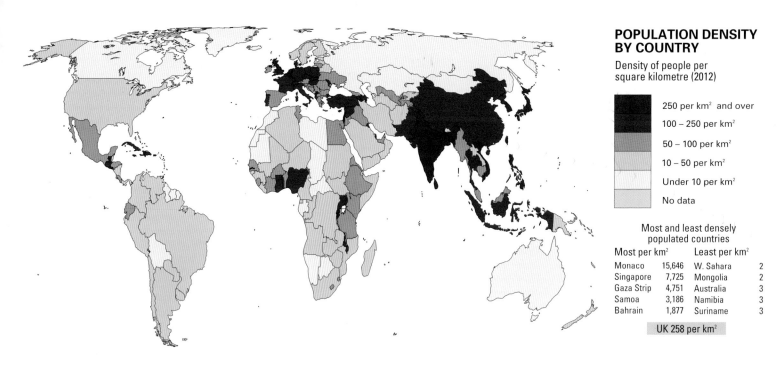

POPULATION DENSITY BY COUNTRY

Density of people per square kilometre (2012)

- 250 per km² and over
- 100 – 250 per km²
- 50 – 100 per km²
- 10 – 50 per km²
- Under 10 per km²
- No data

Most and least densely populated countries

Most per km²		Least per km²	
Monaco	15,646	W. Sahara	2
Singapore	7,725	Mongolia	2
Gaza Strip	4,751	Australia	3
Samoa	3,186	Namibia	3
Bahrain	1,877	Suriname	3

UK 258 per km²

POPULATION CHANGE

Expected change in total population (2004–2050)

- Over 125% gain
- 100 – 125% gain
- 50 – 100% gain
- 25 – 50% gain
- 0 – 25% gain
- No change or loss

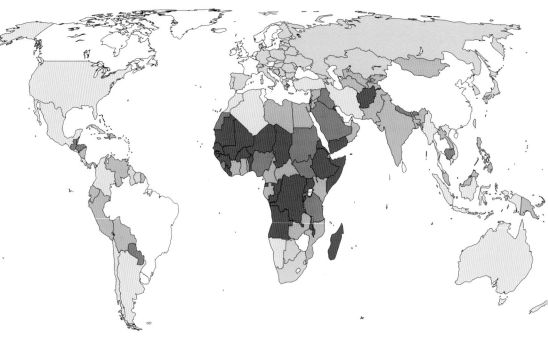

Based on estimates for the year 2050, the ten most populous nations in the world will be, in millions:

India	1,628	Pakistan	295
China	1,437	Bangladesh	280
USA	420	Brazil	221
Indonesia	308	Congo Dem. Rep.	181
Nigeria	307	Ethiopia	171

UK (2050) 77 million

URBAN POPULATION

Percentage of total population living in towns and cities (2010)

- 80% urban and over
- 60 – 80% urban
- 40 – 60% urban
- 20 – 40% urban
- Under 20% urban
- No data

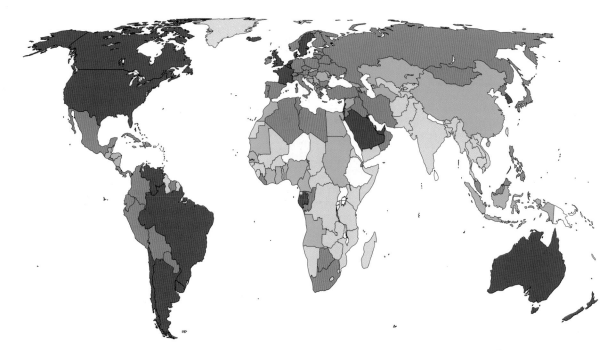

Countries that are the most and least urbanized (%)

Most urbanized		Least urbanized	
Singapore	100	Burundi	11
Kuwait	98	Papua N. Guinea	13
Belgium	97	Uganda	13

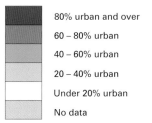

UK 80% urban

In 2008, for the first time in history, more than half the world's population lived in urban areas.

POPULATION BY CONTINENT

In this diagram the size of each continent is in proportion to its population (2011).

Each square represents 10 million people.

Population of countries (2012)
Top 20 countries (millions)

China	1,343
India	1,205
USA	314
Indonesia	249
Brazil	199
Pakistan	190
Nigeria	170
Bangladesh	161
Russia	143
Japan	127
Mexico	115
Philippines	104
Vietnam	92
Ethiopia	91
Egypt	84
Germany	81
Turkey	80
Iran	79
Congo, Dem. Rep.	74
Thailand	67

UK 63 million

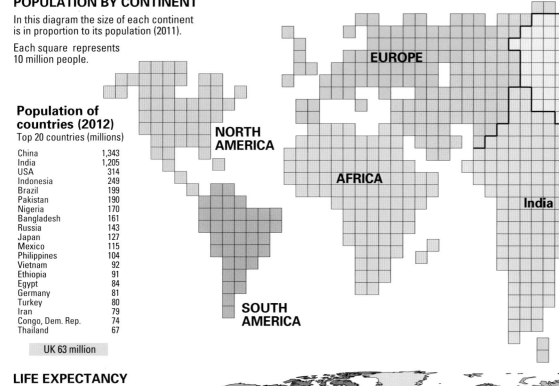

LIFE EXPECTANCY

The average expected lifespan of babies born in 2010

- Over 80 years
- 70 – 80 years
- 60 – 70 years
- 50 – 60 years
- Under 50 years
- No data

Countries with the highest and lowest life expectancy at birth in years

Highest		Lowest	
Australia	82	Angola	39
Italy	82	Afghanistan	45
Japan	82	Nigeria	48
Singapore	82	Chad	48
Canada	81	South Africa	49

UK 80 years

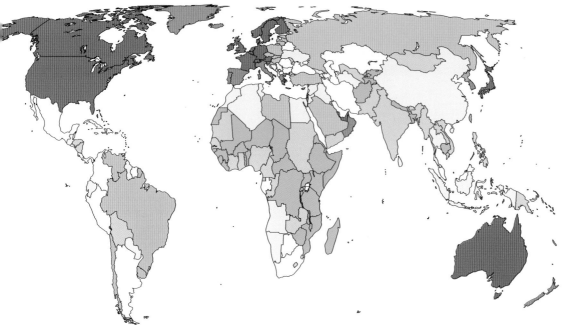

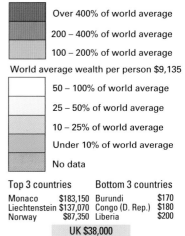

WEALTH

The value of total production in 2010 divided by the population (the Gross National Income per capita)

- Over 400% of world average
- 200 – 400% of world average
- 100 – 200% of world average

World average wealth per person $9,135

- 50 – 100% of world average
- 25 – 50% of world average
- 10 – 25% of world average
- Under 10% of world average
- No data

Top 3 countries		Bottom 3 countries	
Monaco	$183,150	Burundi	$170
Liechtenstein	$137,070	Congo (D. Rep.)	$180
Norway	$87,350	Liberia	$200

UK $38,000

COPYRIGHT PHILIP'S

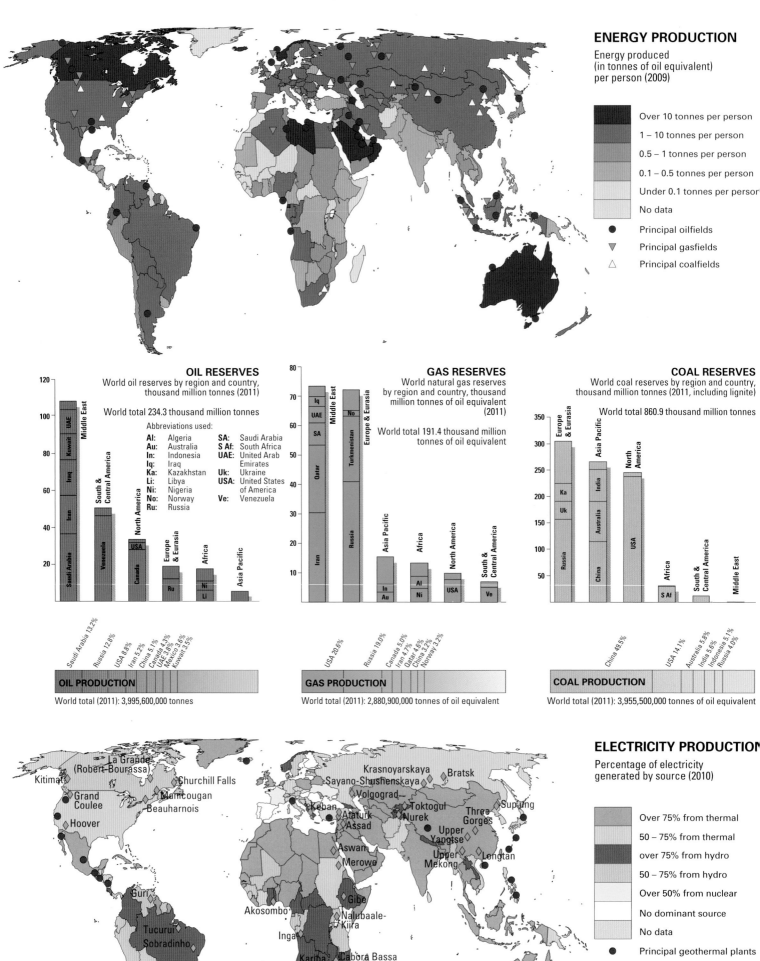

ENERGY PRODUCTION

Energy produced
(in tonnes of oil equivalent)
per person (2009)

- Over 10 tonnes per person
- 1 – 10 tonnes per person
- 0.5 – 1 tonnes per person
- 0.1 – 0.5 tonnes per person
- Under 0.1 tonnes per person
- No data

- ● Principal oilfields
- ▽ Principal gasfields
- △ Principal coalfields

OIL RESERVES

World oil reserves by region and country,
thousand million tonnes (2011)

World total 234.3 thousand million tonnes

Abbreviations used:

Al:	Algeria	SA:	Saudi Arabia
Au:	Australia	S Af:	South Africa
In:	Indonesia	UAE:	United Arab
Iq:	Iraq		Emirates
Ka:	Kazakhstan	Uk:	Ukraine
Li:	Libya	USA:	United States
Ni:	Nigeria		of America
No:	Norway	Ve:	Venezuela
Ru:	Russia		

OIL PRODUCTION

Saudi Arabia 13.2% · Russia 12.8% · USA 8.8% · Iran 5.2% · China 5.1% · Canada 4.3% · UAE 3.8% · Mexico 3.6% · Kuwait 3.5%

World total (2011): 3,995,600,000 tonnes

GAS RESERVES

World natural gas reserves
by region and country, thousand
million tonnes of oil equivalent
(2011)

World total 191.4 thousand million
tonnes of oil equivalent

GAS PRODUCTION

USA 20.6% · Russia 19.0% · Canada 5.0% · Iran 4.7% · Qatar 4.6% · China 3.2% · Norway 3.2%

World total (2011): 2,880,900,000 tonnes of oil equivalent

COAL RESERVES

World coal reserves by region and country,
thousand million tonnes (2011, including lignite)

World total 860.9 thousand million tonnes

COAL PRODUCTION

China 49.5% · USA 14.1% · Australia 5.8% · India 5.6% · Indonesia 5.1% · Russia 4.0%

World total (2011): 3,955,500,000 tonnes of oil equivalent

ELECTRICITY PRODUCTION

Percentage of electricity
generated by source (2010)

- Over 75% from thermal
- 50 – 75% from thermal
- over 75% from hydro
- 50 – 75% from hydro
- Over 50% from nuclear
- No dominant source
- No data

- ● Principal geothermal plants
- ◆ Principal hydroelectric plant

FOOD PRODUCTION

- Principal fishing areas
- Nomadic herding
- Forestry
- Hunting, fishing and gathering
- Subsistence agriculture (growing food to feed the family)
- Livestock ranching (large-scale breeding and rearing of animals for sale)
- Commercial farming (arable land, dairying, and small-scale grazing to produce food for sale)
- Urban areas (commercial, industrial and residential land use)
- Unproductive land

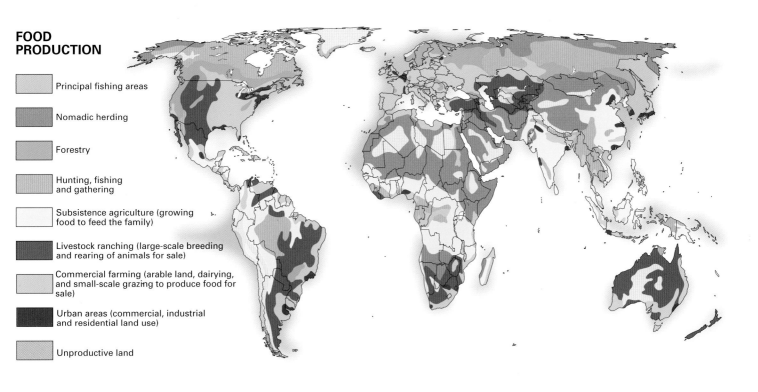

DAILY FOOD CONSUMPTION

Average daily food intake in calories per person (2009)

- Over 3,500 calories
- 3,000 – 3,500 calories
- 2,500 – 3,000 calories
- 2,000 – 2,500 calories
- Under 2,000 calories
- No data

Top 5 countries		Bottom 5 countries	
Austria	3,819	Afghanistan	1,539
USA	3,748	Congo (Dem. Rep.)	1,605
Greece	3,725	Eritrea	1,605
Belgium	3,694	Burundi	1,685
Luxembourg	3,681	Somalia	1,744

UK 3,458

In 2010, the United Nations estimated that 868 million people (almost one in seven) were undernourished, worldwide.

WATER SUPPLY

The percentage of total population with access to safe drinking water (2008)

- Over 90% with safe water
- 80 – 90% with safe water
- 70 – 80% with safe water
- Under 70% with safe water
- No data

Least well-provided countries

Western Sahara	26%
Somalia	30%
Ethiopia	38%
Madagascar	41%
Papua New Guinea	41%
Equatorial Guinea	43%

One person in eight in the world has no access to a safe water supply.

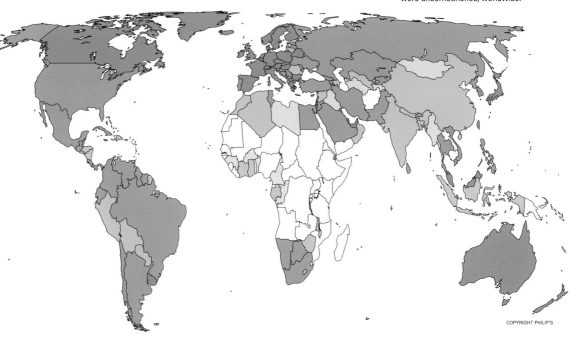

COPYRIGHT PHILIP'S

WORLD TRADE

The percentage share of total
world exports by value (2011)

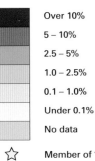

	Over 10%
	5 – 10%
	2.5 – 5%
	1.0 – 2.5%
	0.1 – 1.0%
	Under 0.1%
	No data
☆	Member of 'G8'

*The members of 'G8' account
for more than half the total trade.
The majority of nations contribute
less than one quarter of 1% to
the worldwide total of exports;
EU countries account for over 30%;
the Pacific Rim nations over 45%.*

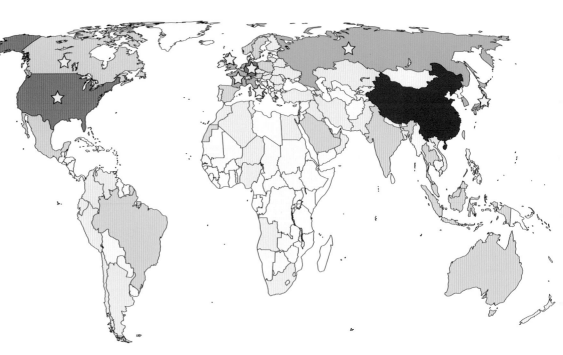

INTERNET USERS

The percentage of
total population
using the internet (2009)

	Over 75% use the internet
	50 – 75% use the internet
	25 – 50% use the internet
	10 – 25% use the internet
	Under 10% use the intern
	No data

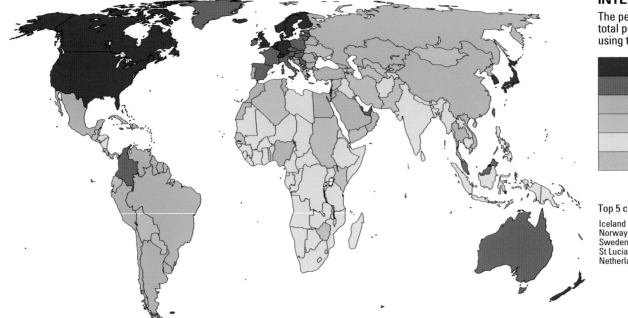

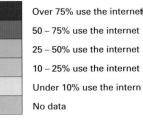

Top 5 countries		Bottom 5 countr	
Iceland	98%	East Timor	0.
Norway	95%	Burma	0.
Sweden	93%	Sierra Leone	0.
St Lucia	89%	Congo (D. Rep.)	0.
Netherlands	89%	Bangladesh	0.

UK 84%

INTERNATIONAL AID

Official Development
Assistance (ODA) provided
and received, US$ per
person (2010)

	Over $250	
	$100 – $250	PROVIDERS ↑
	$50 – $100	
	Under $10	RECEIVERS ↓
	$10 – $50	
	$50 – $100	
	Over $100	
	No data	

Top 5 providers		Top 5 receivers	
Norway	$975	Tuvalu	$1,785
Luxembourg	$806	Palau	$1,737
Denmark	$522	Marshall Is	$1,101
Sweden	$498	Micronesia	$1,093
Netherlands	$378	Gaza Strip	$748

UK provides $208

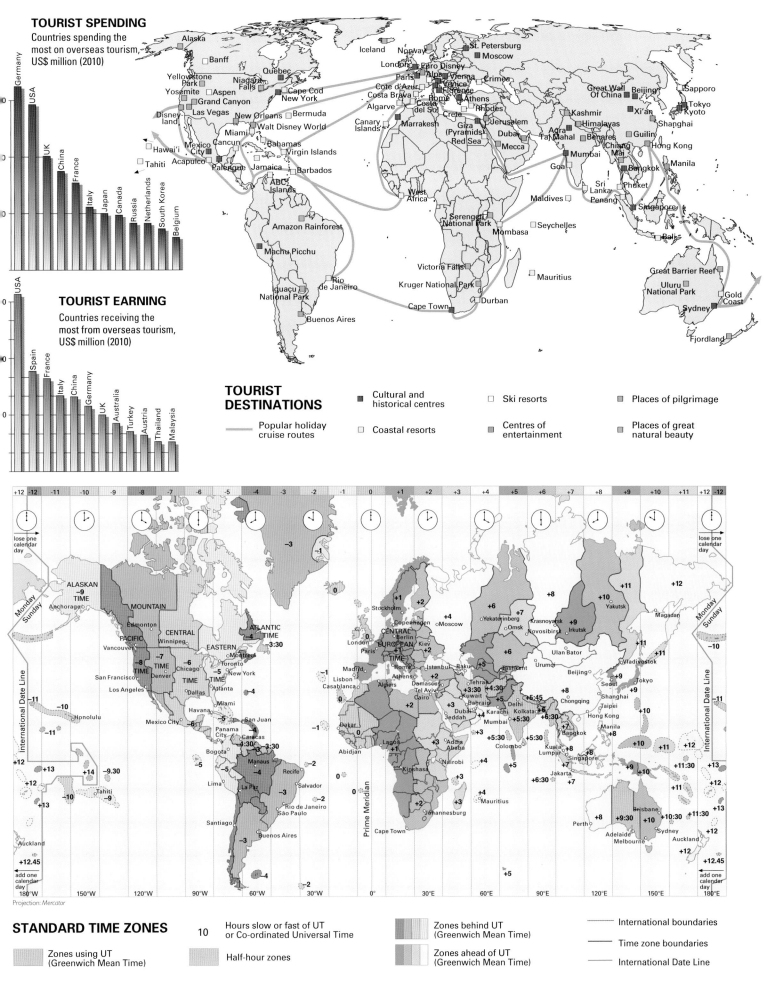

TOURIST SPENDING
Countries spending the most on overseas tourism, US$ million (2010)

TOURIST EARNING
Countries receiving the most from overseas tourism, US$ million (2010)

TOURIST DESTINATIONS

- Cultural and historical centres
- Popular holiday cruise routes
- Coastal resorts
- Ski resorts
- Centres of entertainment
- Places of pilgrimage
- Places of great natural beauty

STANDARD TIME ZONES

10 Hours slow or fast of UT or Co-ordinated Universal Time

- Zones using UT (Greenwich Mean Time)
- Half-hour zones
- Zones behind UT (Greenwich Mean Time)
- Zones ahead of UT (Greenwich Mean Time)
- International boundaries
- Time zone boundaries
- International Date Line

Projection: Mercator

The Earth rotates through 360° in 24 hours, and so moves 15° every hour. The World is divided into 24 standard time zones, each centred on lines of longitude at 15° intervals. The Greenwich Meridian (or Prime Meridian) lies on the centre of the first zone. All places to the west of Greenwich are one hour behind for every 15° of longitude; places to the east are ahead by one hour for every 15°.

COPYRIGHT PHILIP'S

FLAG	COUNTRY	CAPITAL CITY	AREA	POPULATION	POPULATION CHANGE	BIRTHS	DEATHS	LIFE EXPECTANCY	INCOME
			thousand square kilometres	million people	percent per year	per thousand people	per thousand people	years	US $ per person
			2012	2012	2012	2012	2012	2012	2011
	Afghanistan	Kabul	652	30.4	2.2	39	15	50	1,000
	Albania	Tirane	28.7	3.0	0.3	12	6	78	7,800
	Algeria	Algiers	2,382	37.4	1.9	24	4	75	7,200
	Angola	Luanda	1,247	18.1	2.8	39	12	55	5,900
	Argentina	Buenos Aires	2,780	42.2	1.0	17	7	77	17,400
	Armenia	Yerevan	29.8	3.0	0.1	13	8	73	5,400
	Australia	Canberra	7,741	22.0	1.1	12	7	82	40,800
	Austria	Vienna	83.9	8.2	0.0	9	10	80	41,700
	Azerbaijan	Baku	86.6	9.5	1.0	17	7	71	10,200
	Bahamas	Nassau	13.9	0.3	0.9	16	7	71	30,900
	Bahrain	Manama	0.7	1.2	2.7	14	3	78	27,300
	Bangladesh	Dhaka	144	161.1	1.6	23	6	70	1,700
	Barbados	Bridgetown	0.4	0.3	0.4	12	8	75	23,600
	Belarus	Minsk	208	9.6	-0.2	11	14	71	14,900
	Belgium	Brussels	30.5	10.4	0.1	10	11	80	37,600
	Belize	Belmopan	23.0	0.3	2.0	26	6	68	8,300
	Benin	Porto-Novo	113	9.6	2.9	38	9	60	1,500
	Bhutan	Thimphu	47.0	0.7	1.2	19	7	68	6,000
	Bolivia	La Paz/Sucre	1,099	10.3	1.7	24	7	68	4,800
	Bosnia-Herzegovina	Sarajevo	51.2	3.9	-0.1	9	9	79	8,200
	Botswana	Gaborone	582	2.1	1.5	22	12	56	16,300
	Brazil	Brasília	8,514	199.3	0.9	15	7	73	11,600
	Brunei	Bandar Seri Begawan	5.8	0.4	1.7	18	3	76	49,400
	Bulgaria	Sofia	111	7.0	-0.8	9	14	74	13,500
	Burkina Faso	Ouagadougou	274	17.3	3.1	43	12	54	1,500
	Burma	Rangoon/Naypyidaw	677	54.6	1.1	19	8	65	1,300
	Burundi	Bujumbura	27.8	10.6	3.1	41	9	59	400
	Cambodia	Phnom Penh	181	15.0	1.7	25	8	63	2,300
	Cameroon	Yaoundé	475	20.1	2.1	32	12	55	2,300
	Canada	Ottawa	9,971	34.3	0.8	10	8	81	40,300
	Cape Verde Islands	Praia	4.0	0.5	1.4	21	6	71	4,000
	Central African Republic	Bangui	623	5.1	2.1	36	15	50	800
	Chad	N'djamena	1,284	11.0	2.0	39	15	49	1,900
	Chile	Santiago	757	17.1	0.9	14	6	78	16,100
	China	Beijing	9,597	1343.2	0.5	12	7	75	8,400
	Colombia	Bogotá	1,139	45.2	1.1	17	5	75	10,100
	Congo	Brazzaville	342	4.4	2.8	40	11	55	4,600
	Congo (Dem. Rep.)	Kinshasa	2,345	73.6	2.6	37	11	56	300
	Costa Rica	San José	51.1	4.6	1.3	16	4	78	11,500
	Croatia	Zagreb	56.5	4.5	-0.1	10	12	76	18,300
	Cuba	Havana	111	11.1	-0.1	10	8	78	9,900
	Cyprus	Nicosia	9.3	1.1	1.6	11	6	78	29,100
	Czech Republic	Prague	78.9	10.2	-0.1	9	11	77	25,900

FLAG	COUNTRY	CAPITAL CITY	AREA thousand square kilometres 2012	POPULATION million people 2012	POPULATION CHANGE percent per year 2012	BIRTHS per thousand people 2012	DEATHS per thousand people 2012	LIFE EXPECTANCY years 2012	INCOME US $ per person 2011
	Denmark	Copenhagen	43.1	5.5	0.2	10	10	79	40,200
	Djibouti	Djibouti	23.2	0.8	2.3	25	8	62	2,600
	Dominican Republic	Santo Domingo	48.5	10.1	1.3	19	4	77	9,300
	East Timor	Dili	14.9	1.1	2.5	35	6	68	3,100
	Ecuador	Quito	284	15.2	1.4	20	5	76	8,300
	Egypt	Cairo	1,001	83.7	1.9	24	5	73	6,500
	El Salvador	San Salvador	21.0	6.1	0.3	17	6	74	7,600
	Equatorial Guinea	Malabo	28.1	0.7	2.6	35	9	63	19,300
	Eritrea	Asmara	118	6.1	2.5	32	8	63	700
	Estonia	Tallinn	45.1	1.3	-0.7	10	14	74	20,200
	Ethiopia	Addis Ababa	1,104	91.2	2.9	39	9	57	1,100
	Fiji	Suva	18.3	0.9	0.8	21	6	72	4,600
	Finland	Helsinki	338	5.3	0.1	10	10	79	38,300
	France	Paris	552	65.6	0.5	13	9	81	35,000
	Gabon	Libreville	268	1.6	2.0	35	13	52	16,000
	Gambia	Banjul	11.3	1.8	2.3	33	8	64	2,100
	Georgia	Tbilisi	69.7	4.6	-0.3	11	10	77	5,400
	Germany	Berlin	357	81.3	-0.2	8	11	80	37,900
	Ghana	Accra	239	24.7	2.2	32	8	61	3,100
	Greece	Athens	132	10.8	0.1	9	11	80	27,600
	Guatemala	Guatemala	109	14.1	1.9	26	5	71	5,000
	Guinea	Conakry	246	10.9	2.6	37	10	59	1,100
	Guinea-Bissau	Bissau	36.1	1.6	2.0	35	15	49	1,100
	Guyana	Georgetown	215	0.7	-0.3	17	7	67	7,500
	Haiti	Port-au-Prince	27.8	9.8	0.9	24	8	63	1,200
	Honduras	Tegucigalpa	112	8.3	1.8	25	5	71	4,300
	Hungary	Budapest	93.0	10.0	-0.2	9	13	75	19,600
	Iceland	Reykjavik	103	0.3	0.7	13	7	81	38,000
	India	New Delhi	3,287	1,205.1	1.3	21	7	67	3,700
	Indonesia	Jakarta	1,905	248.6	1.0	18	6	72	4,700
	Iran	Tehrān	1,648	78.9	1.2	19	6	70	12,200
	Iraq	Baghdād	438	31.1	2.3	28	5	71	3,900
	Ireland	Dublin	70.3	4.7	1.1	16	6	80	39,500
	Israel	Jerusalem	20.6	7.6	1.5	19	6	81	31,000
	Italy	Rome	301	61.3	0.4	9	10	82	30,100
	Ivory Coast	Yamoussoukro	322	22.0	2.0	30	10	57	1,600
	Jamaica	Kingston	11.0	2.9	0.7	19	7	73	9,000
	Japan	Tokyo	378	127.4	-0.1	8	9	84	34,300
	Jordan	Amman	89.3	6.5	-1.0	27	3	80	5,900
	Kazakhstan	Astana	2,725	17.5	1.2	20	9	70	13,000
	Kenya	Nairobi	580	43.0	2.4	32	7	63	1,700
	Korea, North	P'yŏngyang	121	24.6	0.5	15	9	69	1,800
	Korea, South	Seoul	99.3	48.9	0.2	8	6	79	31,700

FLAG	COUNTRY	CAPITAL CITY	AREA thousand square kilometres 2012	POPULATION million people 2012	POPULATION CHANGE percent per year 2012	BIRTHS per thousand people 2012	DEATHS per thousand people 2012	LIFE EXPECTANCY years 2012	INCOME US $ per person 2011
	Kosovo	Priština	10.9	1.8	-	-	-	75	6,500
	Kuwait	Kuwait	17.8	2.6	1.9	21	2	77	40,700
	Kyrgyzstan	Bishkek	200	5.5	0.9	24	7	69	2,400
	Laos	Vientiane	237	6.6	1.7	26	8	63	2,700
	Latvia	Riga	64.6	2.2	-0.6	10	14	73	15,400
	Lebanon	Beirut	10.4	4.1	-0.4	15	7	75	15,600
	Lesotho	Maseru	30.4	1.9	0.3	27	15	52	1,400
	Liberia	Monrovia	111	3.9	2.6	36	10	57	400
	Libya	Tripoli	1,760	5.6	2.0	18	5	78	14,100
	Lithuania	Vilnius	65.2	3.5	-0.3	9	11	76	18,700
	Luxembourg	Luxembourg	2.6	0.5	1.1	12	9	80	84,700
	Macedonia	Skopje	25.7	2.1	0.2	12	9	75	10,400
	Madagascar	Antananarivo	587	22.0	2.7	34	7	64	900
	Malawi	Lilongwe	118	16.3	2.8	40	13	52	900
	Malaysia	Kuala Lumpur/ Putrajaya	330	29.2	1.5	21	5	74	15,600
	Mali	Bamako	1,240	15.5	3.0	47	14	53	1,300
	Malta	Valletta	0.3	0.4	0.4	10	9	80	25,700
	Mauritania	Nouakchott	1,026	3.4	2.3	33	9	62	2,200
	Mauritius	Port Louis	2.0	1.3	0.7	14	7	75	15,000
	Mexico	Mexico City	1,958	115.0	1.1	19	5	77	15,100
	Moldova	Kishinev	33.9	3.7	-1.0	13	13	70	3,400
	Mongolia	Ulan Bator	1,567	3.2	1.5	21	6	90	4,500
	Montenegro	Podgorica	14.0	0.7	-0.6	11	9	69	11,200
	Morocco	Rabat	447	32.3	1.1	19	5	73	5,100
	Mozambique	Maputo	802	23.5	2.4	39	13	52	1,100
	Namibia	Windhoek	824	2.2	0.8	21	13	52	7,300
	Nepal	Katmandu	147	29.9	1.8	22	7	67	1,300
	Netherlands	Amsterdam/ The Hague	41.5	16.7	0.5	11	8	81	42,300
	New Zealand	Wellington	271	4.3	0.9	14	7	81	27,900
	Nicaragua	Managua	130	5.7	1.1	19	5	72	3,200
	Niger	Niamey	1,267	16.3	3.4	48	13	54	800
	Nigeria	Abuja	924	170.1	2.6	39	13	52	2,600
	Norway	Oslo	324	4.7	0.3	11	9	80	53,300
	Oman	Muscat	310	3.1	2.0	24	3	74	26,200
	Pakistan	Islamabad	796	190.3	1.6	24	7	66	2,800
	Panama	Panamá	75.5	3.5	1.4	19	5	78	13,600
	Papua New Guinea	Port Moresby	463	6.3	1.9	26	7	66	2,500
	Paraguay	Asunción	407	6.5	1.3	17	5	76	5,500
	Peru	Lima	1,285	29.6	1.0	19	6	73	10,000
	Philippines	Manila	300	103.8	1.9	25	5	72	4,100
	Poland	Warsaw	323	38.4	-0.1	10	10	76	20,100
	Portugal	Lisbon	88.8	10.8	0.2	10	11	79	23,200
	Qatar	Doha	11.0	2.0	4.9	10	2	78	102,700

FLAG	COUNTRY	CAPITAL CITY	AREA thousand square kilometres 2012	POPULATION million people 2012	POPULATION CHANGE percent per year 2012	BIRTHS per thousand people 2012	DEATHS per thousand people 2012	LIFE EXPECTANCY years 2012	INCOME US $ per person 2011
	Romania	Bucharest	238	21.8	-0.3	9	12	74	12,300
	Russia	Moscow	17,075	142.5	-0.0	12	14	66	16,700
	Rwanda	Kigali	26.3	11.7	2.8	36	10	58	1,300
	Saudi Arabia	Riyadh	2,150	26.5	1.5	19	3	74	24,000
	Senegal	Dakar	197	13.0	2.5	36	9	60	1,900
	Serbia	Belgrade	77.5	7.3	-0.5	9	14	75	10,700
	Sierra Leone	Freetown	71.7	5.5	2.3	38	11	57	800
	Singapore	Singapore	0.7	5.4	2.0	8	3	84	59,900
	Slovakia	Bratislava	49.0	5.5	0.1	10	10	76	23,400
	Slovenia	Ljubljana	20.3	2.0	-0.2	9	11	77	29,100
	Solomon Islands	Honiara	28.9	0.6	2.2	27	4	74	3,300
	Somalia	Mogadishu	638	10.1	1.6	42	15	51	600
	South Africa	Cape Town/ Pretoria	1,221	48.8	-0.4	19	17	49	11,000
	South Sudan	Juba	620	10.6	-	-	-	-	1,546
	Spain	Madrid	498	47.0	0.7	10	9	82	30,600
	Sri Lanka	Colombo	65.6	21.5	0.9	17	6	76	5,600
	Sudan	Khartoum	1,886	34.2	1.9	32	8	83	3,000
	Suriname	Paramaribo	163	0.6	1.2	17	6	71	9,500
	Swaziland	Mbabane	17.4	1.4	1.2	26	14	49	5,200
	Sweden	Stockholm	450	9.1	0.2	10	10	81	40,600
	Switzerland	Berne	41.3	7.9	0.9	10	8	81	43,400
	Syria	Damascus	185	22.5	-0.8	24	4	75	5,100
	Taiwan	Taipei	36.0	23.2	0.3	9	7	78	37,900
	Tajikistan	Dushanbe	143	7.8	1.8	26	6	66	2,000
	Tanzania	Dodoma	945	46.9	2.9	38	9	53	1,500
	Thailand	Bangkok	513	67.1	0.5	13	7	74	9,700
	Togo	Lomé	56.8	7.0	2.7	35	8	63	900
	Trinidad and Tobago	Port of Spain	5.1	1.2	-0.1	14	8	72	20,300
	Tunisia	Tunis	164	10.7	1.0	17	6	75	9,500
	Turkey	Ankara	775	79.7	1.2	18	6	73	14,600
	Turkmenistan	Ashkhabad	488	5.1	1.1	20	6	69	7,500
	Uganda	Kampala	241	33.6	3.3	46	12	53	1,300
	Ukraine	Kiev	604	44.9	-0.6	10	16	69	7,200
	United Arab Emirates	Abu Dhabi	83.6	5.3	3.1	16	2	77	48,500
	United Kingdom	London	242	63.0	0.6	12	9	80	35,900
	USA	Washington D.C.	9,629	313.8	0.9	14	8	78	48,100
	Uruguay	Montevideo	175	3.3	0.2	13	10	76	15,400
	Uzbekistan	Tashkent	447	28.4	0.9	17	5	73	3,300
	Venezuela	Caracas	912	28.0	1.5	20	5	74	12,400
	Vietnam	Hanoi	332	91.5	1.1	17	6	72	3,300
	Yemen	Sana	528	24.8	2.6	33	7	64	2,500
	Zambia	Lusaka	753	13.8	2.9	43	13	53	1,600
	Zimbabwe	Harare	391	12.6	4.4	32	12	52	500

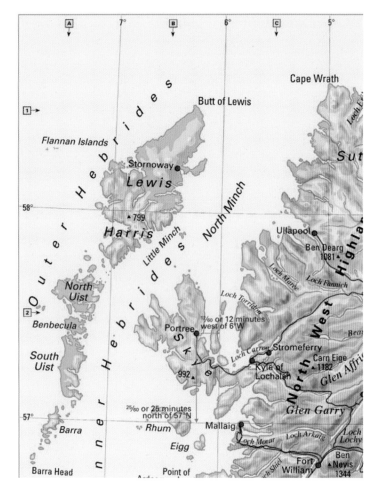

This index contains the names of all the principal places and features shown on the maps in the atlas. They are listed in alphabetical order. If a name has a description as part of it, for example, Bay of Biscay, the name is in alphabetical order, followed by the description:

Biscay, Bay of ......

Sometimes, the same name occurs in more than one country. In these cases, the country names are added after each place name. For example:

Córdoba, *Argentina* ..
Córdoba, *Spain* .....

All rivers are indexed to their mouths or confluences and are followed by the symbol →. All country names are followed by the symbol ■.

Each place name is followed by its latitude and longitude, and then its map page number and figure-letter grid reference. Both latitude and longitude are measured in degrees and minutes. There are 60 minutes in a degree. The latitude is followed by N(orth) or S(outh) and the longitude by E(ast) or W(est). The map extract on the left shows how to find a place by estimating the required distance from the nearest line of latitude or longitude on the map page. Portree is used as an example:

Portree .... 57°25'N 6°12'W **18 2B**

There are 60 minutes between the lines and so to find the position of Portree an estimate has to be made. 25 parts of the 60 minutes north of the 57°N latitude line, and 12 parts of the 60 minutes west of the 6°W longitude line.

The latitude and longitude are followed by a number in bold type which refers to the number of the map page on which the place or feature appears. Portree is on page **18**.

The figure and letter which follow the page number give the grid rectangle on the map within which the place or feature appears. The grid is formed by the lines of latitude and longitude. The columns are labelled at the top and bottom of the map with a letter and the rows at the sides of the map with a number. Portree is in the grid square where row **2** crosses column **B**.